Virginia Bakery

REMEMBERED

Virginia Bakery

REMEMBERED

by : TOM THIE &
CYNTHIA BEISCHEL

Charleston — London

THE
History
PRESS

Published by The History Press
Charleston, SC 29403
www.historypress.net

All food photography by Kristin Ungerecht.

First published 2010
Second printing 2010
Third printing 2011

Manufactured in the United States

ISBN 978.1.60949.114.7

Library of Congress Cataloging-in-Publication Data

Beischel, Cynthia Kuhn.
Virginia Bakery remembered / Cynthia Beischel and Tom Thie.
p. cm.
Includes bibliographical references and index.
ISBN 978-1-60949-114-7
1. Baking--Ohio--Cincinnati. 2. Virginia Bakery (Cincinnati, Ohio)--History. 3.
Bakeries--Ohio--Cincinnati--History. I. Thie, Tom (Thomas), 1958- II. Title.
TX763.B375 2010
664'.752--dc22
2010033586

This book is dedicated to our great-grandparents, grandparents and parents and the German heritage they bestowed upon us.

Contents

Acknowledgements   9
Tom's Introduction   11
Cynthia's Introduction   17
The Generations of Thie Bakers in Cincinnati   23

To Be a Thie   25
Shop Stories   70
Before You Bake   90
Schnecken   95
Coffee Cakes   106
Breakfast Rolls   129
Fillings, Frostings and Other Toppings   138
Front Shop Recipes   145
Cakes   154
Pies   167
Doughnuts   177
Cookies   183
Breads   198
Dinner Rolls   210

Virginia Bakery Employees   217
List of Contributors   219
Bibliography   235
Index   237
About the Authors   240

Acknowledgements

Creating *Virginia Bakery Remembered* has been a work of love—a love of quality bakery goods and a love of German heritage—and many people played a part in the process of turning an idea into this beautiful, engaging and useful book.

First, I want to thank Tom Thie. If he hadn't believed in this project, it wouldn't have happened. I was amazed by his generosity—not only in the hours spent working on adapting commercial-size recipes to ones that will work in a home kitchen, but also in the quantity of recipes he produced. His colossal efforts now allow us to make our favorite Virginia Bakery products that we have sorely missed.

I also want to thank all of the Thie family members who opened their hearts and albums for me. I appreciate that they took the time to speak with me and to look up old family information, as well as provide wonderful vintage photos. Getting to know everyone was a pleasure.

Additional thanks go to my daughters, who both contributed significantly. Merritt (Beischel) came to my house many times and took on the duties of cook, house cleaner, laundress, pet sitter, gofer and occasional researcher so I could work full steam ahead on the manuscript. Lindsay (Miklos), who lives in another city, avoided those jobs but helped when I had computer or Internet problems, and her crowning contribution was finding an Internet link that directed me to The History Press.

Staying still in the family, I want to thank my mother-in-law, Rosemary Beischel, for her help with testing recipes. For the past forty years, she has stood out in my mind as a wonderful cook and baker, so I was very pleased when she agreed to put her expertise to work toward helping with this project.

Luckily, I have a very gifted friend, Kristina Strom, who played a dual role. Similar to my German family history in which my ancestors had a bakery, Kristina's Swedish grandfather was a baker. Unlike me, she has always baked from scratch and has a wealth of information in her head about the process. For that reason, she was my obvious choice for the other test baker. Kristina combined that knowledge with her editing skills and had many opportunities to use her red pen.

Fairly early on in our work schedule, I was fortunate enough to find Kristin Ungerecht. Tom and I were both pleased with her photographic work and her ability to capture mouthwatering photos of the baked goods that enhance the recipes.

In the midst of a very tight time frame, Rachel Schmid generously offered to help just when I was trying to figure out what to do with the vintage photos. Having scanned old photos for two other publications about historic subject matters, she saved the day.

And finally, but certainly not without importance, thanks go to the girls at Pink Ink Design Group. Jenna Schweizer and Karen Brown were always willing to help with graphic issues at the eleventh hour.

Without all of you, this book would not be the success that it is. Danke schön.

Cynthia

Besides my family, I would like to thank all the fine employees who put in countless hours of work and tremendous amounts of dedication. I would also like to thank the numerous and devoted customers who came to the bakery over the years. I would particularly like to thank Cynthia Beischel—without her devotion and tireless efforts, this book would not exist. You all are the true gems in my life. I hope your memories are as fond as mine.

Tom

Tom's Introduction

When asked to write this book, I was hesitant. I was aware of the work involved. The photography, gathering information, adjusting recipes, test baking, writing and editing would take countless hours. After much prodding and pleading, I knew it was time to share the stories and recipes of Virginia Bakery, a substantial part of Cincinnati history and, for me, my entire life. As I looked at the food-stained, handwritten, timeworn recipe cards and books of The Bakery, I realized how fragile the connection was. Being the sole custodian of years of baking knowledge, I felt a real need to pass on these recipes. What a shame it would be to lose these to time. The recipes have been handed down in their original form. As best as I could, I have recalibrated them to work in the home kitchen. So here they are. Please use them a lot and keep them well.

The building at 286 Ludlow Avenue was more than a bakery to me; it was my home and my life. I watched family and friends live, laugh, love and die there. My daughter's first bed was there, as well as my mother's last. The year 2005 was an extremely sad one, as I was forced to close the doors forever. I felt I had failed the customers and that it was all over for me as well. Good times no more. But I was down, not out. After a lot of hard work, I'm back, and this book has given me a new purpose. I thank you all for that.

I was extremely proud to be Virginia Bakery, for many good reasons. Not only was quality a way of life there, but it was also our reputation. What a heritage. I grew up among men who were not only proud to be German but even prouder to be American. I'll never forget the day Fritz Pieper cried as they played the National Anthem on the radio before a Reds game. Few know that Virginia Bakery produced one of the first Certified Master Bakers in the United States, my daddy, Howard. It also produced one of the first certified master cake decorators in the United States, my wife, Maureen. What a sacrifice she made as she put her own career in the health field aside and pursued her new one as an award-winning cake decorator. It also saw a lot of good bakers and some downright extremely fine people.

A lot of people ask me why I chose baking. Let me emphasize choice here. After several career opportunities, I chose to come back to the bakery. The reasons were many. First, I've always liked making people happy with food. No Freudian humor, please. I started cooking at an early age. Yes, I had my own Easy Bake Oven. It was also the dream of many kids to own their own bakery. How cool my classmates thought it was, especially when it was my turn for "Treat Day." Okay, I'm gonna name drop here. I've studied under some of the best, including Chefs Emeril Lagasse and Paul Sturkey and Master Bakers Gunther Behrendt and Howard Thie. There was also my grandfather Bill, whose reputation speaks for itself. I've had the honor of cooking for the Rolling Stones and ZZ Top, a couple of U.S. presidents and countless outstanding customers. I wish I knew how many weddings, birthday parties and holiday dinners Virginia Bakery "attended." Believe me, this thought sustained me several times in the wee hours of the morning. During the Christmas holidays, I had Santa delusions as I watched my elves scurrying frantically about in well-orchestrated chaos. Unlike most of my counterparts, I loved the holidays. The smiles on the little faces as you handed them their cookies were part of the magic. It was also a job that made me wealthy—not necessarily rich, but abundant in friends and good times. We had a sign on the wall that read, "Do what you like and you never have to go to work again." I guess that means I've been retired a long time.

It was hard work, and even though there is a shortage of young bakers, I still caution potential candidates. Training a baker was a lot like raising children. It took a lot of time, patience and understanding, but what a worthwhile project. I watched several young men go through the transition, from feeling like they had nothing to knowing they had something. To this day, I have guys thanking me for what we were able to do together.

All bakers started on the sink, where they learned humility. They were the low man on the totem pole, the butt of all jokes. That position also gave them a chance to learn where everything went as they put it away. After about two weeks, they knew, and we knew, if they wanted to stay. Then our apprentice moved to the finish area. Icing, filling and decorating doughnuts, rolls, coffee cakes, all sorts of new and strange things. This is where they started learning the products and how to identify them. With over three hundred products, there was a lot to learn. "What the @#$% is a winky dink?"

Next came the bench. Here our novice baker started working with the dough and progressed through several different stages from coffee cakes to schnecken. As they acquired new bakery skills, so rose their self-esteem. You could see it in the smiles on their faces. All it took was a "Good job" or "Nice tea rings."

After becoming competent on the bench, our apprentice was expected to learn the oven. Proofing and baking are all about timing, and this is where our baker learned it. Literally, minutes could mean hundreds of dollars, not to mention the ridicule of the younger bakers and "Oh Lord! Don't let the boss find out." I've actually caught novice oven men trying to dumpster their mistakes. I came down one morning and the garbage can was still smoking. As I peered into the can, I found about fifty pounds of burnt cookies. You should have seen the look in the oven man's eyes. I won't name any names. Okay, Roger?

Very few made it through the gauntlet to "mixer," where the recipes were disclosed. Hats off to Dusty, Jerry and Juice, to name a few. These guys had their fingers on the pulse of the bakery. The machine couldn't start, much less run, without them. They were expected to be there every day, and they knew it. Fortunately, by now, the loyalty factor was way up there and this was usually not a problem. These young men were now competent bakers and proud of it.

Let me just say a word about the owners of small businesses and toot my own horn. I've seen several people full of zest and zeal enter the food service business with their heads full of romantic notions from the Food Network. As owners, they soon find out about bookkeeping and how interested Uncle Sam is in their business and how many agencies want to dip their fingers in the pie. They also learn how to do everything in their establishment as they fill in for sick employees. They become sounding boards, painters, secretaries, plumbers, delivery boys, cleaners…the list goes on. There are long hours, holidays are a blur and it can be lonely at the top. Believe me, no one is going to tell them what a good job they're doing. They have to know that in their heart.

What makes an otherwise rational person want to do all this, knowing the failure rate is 95 percent for the first year? It's not money, my friends. It's love. It's about forming a bigger family with employees and, ultimately, your customers. I've heard it compared to the comradeship of battle, and I mean no disrespect to our troops in using this analogy, but it is a good one in many ways. Working in that summer bakery was a lot like being in a submarine without the bulkheads. The heat penetrated everything. It was HOT and close, and tempers could rise exponentially. Then came the holidays. Emeril would say, "You need to have a sense of urgency, boys." In the days before Christmas, one could almost feel the testosterone levels rise in the back shop as the doughboys pulled together for a common goal: the customer. To quote Jerry Armstead, "They worked us to death; we had to give the people what they wanted." Then there came the sense of pride in doing the job right and the fun of victory when it was all over. Yes, we had some great times, and some hard times, which is what bonds people universally. I wouldn't trade a moment of it.

Since I've done both, people often ask me what the difference is between being a chef and a baker. The first thing that comes to mind is the pace. Restaurant cooking is extremely fast paced, the NASCAR of cooking. I remember nights at Commander's Palace in New Orleans cooking over three hundred steaks and chops to order in a three-hour period. Baking, with the exception of holidays, is a much slower animal, more like the turtle of fable fame. It is not concerned with speed but reaches the goal nonetheless. As I recall, the turtle won. So it was with me. I preferred the slower pace of baking. Baking slows your pulse and mindset. You have to wait for the yeast to work, the dough to chill and items to finish baking. If you're obsessed with speed, don't bake. It forces you to take a slow step in time and is particularly enjoyable at home. It can be great done alone but also provides for a lot of family bonding. When I bake in Michigan, the kitchen always fills up. I strongly recommend you take some time out of your fast-paced life, slow down and bake. It's good for your soul.

About mistakes: you're going to make a few. Yes, even you. Heck, the first time I made schnecken at home in my new oven, I set it on fire. See how to put out a fire (page 178). If you make mistakes a learning experience, they are no longer mistakes. Grandpa Bill used to say, "If you don't make no mistakes, you ain't learning nothing." There's a double negative in there somewhere, right? Oh well, you get the gist.

Speaking of mistakes, I need to sidetrack here and say I'm glad that as a nation we are starting to correct some of ours. I'm so glad baking has come full circle. Even in the grocery store, it is getting easier to find quality bakery products. "Death to White Bread and Twinkies" should be our mantra. My daughter loves the saying "The whiter the bread, the sooner you're dead." Demand quality and accept nothing less. After years of dietary mistakes,

I believe we are starting to get back on track by eating the foods of our forefathers and shunning the processed crap the food giants have force fed us. Learn to bake and not only will you eat better, but you will also eat less and enjoy it more.

So this is it, my magnum opus, and an opportunity to share the stories and memories. And when you come right down to it, the memories are what it's all about. I've heard it said that in the end your life flashes by like a movie. I'm sure mine is going to have a lot of bakery pictures in it. What joy that will bring. I'm glad I am able to share it with all of you. These recipes are for my family, which is what you have all become.

Tom

For those of you who wish to contact me directly in order to get online advice, ask questions about the recipes or other bakery-related matters and find additional delicious recipes, please visit www.virginiabakeryremembered.com.

Cynthia's Introduction

For as long as I can remember, my family had a weekly standing order at Virginia Bakery, which was located in the Clifton neighborhood of Cincinnati, Ohio. Rain or shine, we would pick up freshly baked bread, a cinnamon crumb cake, one of the fruit coffee cakes (apple was my favorite), a filled tea ring, a cheese pocket, gems, Danish rolls or doughnuts, bran muffins and anything else that captured our gustatory fancy when we were in the store. To us, Sunday morning meant an array of bakery delights. Thanksgiving and Christmas celebrations always included mouth-watering butter bits, as well as delicious cakes and pies. The holidays would not have been the holidays, or other distinctive events as distinctive, without the irresistible and deservedly renowned schnecken, which was to us the crown jewel of all Virginia Bakery's offerings.

In our childhood years, Mom seldom got no for an answer when she asked my sister and me if we wanted to accompany her on the weekly bakery shopping trip—we wanted to make sure that every option had been carefully considered. To underscore the importance of our order, if for any reason my mother was unable to get to the bakery, my father would fit the trip into his busy schedule. For fifty weeks out of the year, my family stopped in at least once. The Thie family closed the bakery's doors for the other two weeks every August so they could vacation on Torch Lake in Michigan. Fortunately, they put up reminder signs several weeks in advance so we were able to stock up and fill our freezer to tide us over until they returned. After thawing, the pastries tasted as delicious as ever.

One of my most vivid memories is of when I was five years old. I brought my brand-new baby doll, which was extremely lifelike in both size and shape, along with me on one of our weekly visits to the bakery. Rather than stand beside my mother at the counter, in order to play my maternal role I chose a small bench between the water fountain and the door closest to the window display. Sitting there, I could hear the banter and laughter of the ladies behind the counter as they boxed up people's orders and replenished the offerings in the glass-fronted cases. And the ever-present enticing fragrance…at that point in time I was convinced that heaven must smell like Virginia Bakery. When we were leaving the store, my mother told me that another customer had scolded her for giving a child my age the responsibility of holding a newborn. For someone to think I was caring for a newborn told me that I had a very special doll indeed and reinforced my conviction that there was magic in the air at Virginia Bakery.

Almost twenty years later, I sat in the same spot with my mother, this time at a table and chairs arrangement that had long since replaced the bench. I again felt a similar sense of enchantment while we selected my wedding cake. As newlyweds living in Franklin, Ohio, my husband and I made frequent trips to Clifton that always included a visit to Virginia Bakery so we could stock up on our favorite baked goods. The weekly routine resumed once we moved back to Cincinnati, first from our Hyde Park and later our Glendale homes.

Taking our two daughters on the weekly jaunts allowed me to pass on the cheerful legacy of entering the friendly shop that was always filled with that heavenly aroma and the promise of free cookies for the girls while my order was being filled. Just as I had looked forward to those trips as a child, my own daughters now loved accompanying me.

Based on the familiar faces I had seen in the shop over the years and the number of people standing in long lines that snaked their way up Ludlow Avenue in every kind of weather during the peak holiday season, I knew my family and I were not alone in our affection for and attachment to Virginia Bakery. In the mid-1980s, an idea for a book celebrating and capturing the unique essence of the bakery arose in my mind. Shortly thereafter, one day while paying for my assortment of boxed and bagged items, I broached the subject with Maureen "Moe" Thie, who was working the cash register. I told her that if anyone in the family was interested in creating a book about the bakery, I would be more than willing to help with the project. Though nothing ever came of that conversation, my dream remained alive and well.

In retrospect, my book concept had entered into a "proofing" period—much the way in the baking process yeast blooms in warm water before being mixed with the other essential ingredients, and then the blended dough is set aside to rise. Though the dough appears to be merely resting, the chemical activity that goes on during this period is critical to the success or failure of the final product. So it was with this project's activity; clearly, all that was needed was more "proofing" time.

In July 2000, following Tom and Moe Thie's decision to close the full line retail shop of Virginia Bakery, Chuck Martin wrote a heartfelt article for the *Cincinnati Enquirer* titled "Pastry Lovers Lose Old Friend." He described the customers' reactions to the loss of the seventy-three-year-old bakery, a loss that was felt far beyond the reaches of Clifton. In the interview Chuck conducted, Tom stated that he wanted the customers to remember Virginia Bakery "the way it was."

That one little establishment had become so important to so many people in so many ways. People who lived or worked in Clifton and had a history of buying Virginia Bakery products were devastated by the news. Among the loyal customers and employees, emotions ran the gamut from sadness (some people literally wept) to anger when the retail store was closed. Many customers' spirits were lifted when they heard the bakery was still going to make wedding cakes and open up once in a while to sell schnecken. That transition period lasted until 2005, when Tom's injuries from a tree fall forced him to close these services.

In November 2006, Busken Bakery entered negotiations with Tom to make a few of Virginia Bakery's famous trademark pastries, starting with schnecken and later followed by brown-n-serve rolls and butterscotch gems. When the billboards first announced that schnecken would once again be made available, Busken was flooded with orders that could not be kept up with. When I called to complain that I had made five trips over several days to two of their locations and had been unsuccessful in getting there in time to buy one, the woman I spoke with admitted that they had had no idea of the interest that would be generated by this event.

After finally enjoying some of the schnecken, which was pretty close to what I remembered, I decided to call Tom and let him know how much we had appreciated being able to purchase this fondly remembered item. I also took the opportunity to once again mention the book concept. After several months of persistence, Tom finally agreed—the time had come to preserve the bakery's rich, abundant history and create a record of his family's products. The "proofing" period was at long last complete.

I placed the following ad in local newspapers and other venues—the response was overwhelming:

Virginia Bakery—does that name conjure sweet memories? We've been authorized to write a book about the bakery and want to hear from you. How did you discover the place? When was your first visit? How often did you go there, for how many years? What do you most vividly recall? Did Virginia Bakery play a role in family celebrations? What was your favorite baked good? To share your recollections and be considered for an interview, e-mail <u>VirginiaBakeryRemembered@gmail.com</u> or write to PO Box 46844, Cincinnati, OH 45246-0844. Whether or not your story is included, you will be acknowledged in the book.

Before we started this venture, I knew a lot about being a customer but not much beyond that. Contacting and hearing stories from the people who worked where the magic happened was great fun. The Thie family members provided information about family matters and bakery history; former employees shared their memories about the back shops and the retail area in front; and customers ranging in age from their twenties to their nineties told heartfelt stories about their experiences when shopping, as well as indicating what "favorite item" category they fit into.

The impressions of all the folks who responded to my advertisement are included in the chapter essays. Receiving so many similar stories was both amazing and reassuring. Based on our similarly fond recollections, we had definitely all been in the same place—some of us, no doubt, crossing paths when the bakery was in operation. (I was stunned to find out that I was not the only person who had saved and actually framed one of the red-and-white bakery box lids to commemorate the golden days of Virginia Bakery.) Of course, the heart of the bakery was the food, which is now the heart of this book thanks to Tom's generosity. He graciously agreed to provide recipes for over seventy of the Virginia Bakery's most popular items, many of which I rattled off easily by memory when he asked what I'd like to feature in the book. After a great deal of time-consuming work, he recalibrated and scaled down the shop recipes to versions that can be made in the home kitchen.

Virginia Bakery Remembered contains a wealth of wonderful traditional recipes, rich in German heritage, for those who enjoy baking. This book is also for everyone who, like me, loved the bakery and still can't go down Clifton Avenue without yearning to turn the corner onto Ludlow and pull into the bakery's parking lot. Newcomers will learn about why the Virginia Bakery was such a special establishment and holds such a special place in our hearts. The loyal customers who experienced Virginia Bakery always felt, just as the box logo stated, that we had the "very best." This book is the next best thing to being there. For all of you who have said over the years, "Oh, I wish I could just have one more piece of this or that," *Virginia Bakery Remembered* is the answer. With this book, you are given the opportunity to once again relive some of your fondest memories!

Cynthia

The Generations of Thie Bakers in Cincinnati

Franz Wilhelm Thie—born January 21, 1793

Franz Frederich Thie—born December 20, 1819, in Espelkamp, Grossendorf

Heinrich Wilhelm Thie—born April 26, 1850, in Rahden, Germany
married on November 4, 1870, to
Henriette Luise Niehus
They had five sons, one of whom was Wilhelm Frederick Thie

Wilhelm "William" Frederick Thie—born in 1878; died on May 10, 1919
married in 1900 to
Henrietta "Hattie" Louise Pottschmidt—born September 1, 1880; died
January 13, 1963
They had two sons: William Frederick and Carl Henry

William "Bill" Frederick Thie—born January 23, 1904; died July 20, 1978
married on July 1, 1925, to
Myrtle Suhre—born September 17, 1904; died November 13, 1998
They had six children: William Howard, Paul Louis, Ronald Carl, Janet
Esther (Koenig), Sandra Louise (Holzman) and Sharon Elizabeth

William Howard "Howard" Thie—born July 3, 1926; died December 7, 1999
married on May 13, 1950, to
Cordelia "Cindy" Leathers—born April 30, 1928; died August 26, 1993
They had three children: Jennifer Lynn, Deborah Elaine and William Thomas

William Thomas "Tom" Thie—born December 30, 1958
married on June 2, 1990, to
Maureen "Moe" Sheppard—born September 9, 1961
They have one daughter, Carly, born March 9, 1995

To Be a Thie

First Generation of the
Thie Bakery Family in Cincinnati

About 1890, a young ambitious baker in his early twenties named Wilhelm (later Americanized to "William") Frederick Thie immigrated to the United States from Rahden, Germany. In 1900, he married Henrietta "Hattie" Pottschmidt, who had emigrated from Westphalia, Germany, in 1893 at the age of thirteen and had also been part of a bakery family. According to a 1950 interview with Clementine Paddleford for *This Week* (a nationally distributed Sunday newspaper supplement to the *Cincinnati Enquirer*), Hattie and her husband started their first bakery in that same year. They bought the bakery formerly managed by the Pottschmidt sisters. While the exact location of that bakery is not clear, in 1906 the Wm. Thie Baking Co. was recorded as being in the West End area of downtown, near the corner of Liberty and Dudley Streets. This establishment had a "fleet" of four horse-drawn wagons and one motorized vehicle (horse-less carriage) that delivered to twenty-nine outlets in Cincinnati. These outlets were storefronts, typically owned by a couple who sold baked goods on commission under the Wm. Thie name.

In the same article, Hattie reminisced, "In those days, we were downtown and opened at 4:00 in the morning to have breakfast breads fresh from the oven—the ladies would come in and get hot breads for breakfast, one day being as busy as the next." During the later decades, Virginia

Above: The Pottschmidt family back in Germany. Hattie is the little girl standing. Aren't they a fun-looking bunch?

Left: Wilhelm, young Bill and Hattie Thie, circa 1909.

Opposite, top: The Wm. Thie Baking Company included a "high-tech" horseless carriage among the "fleet" of horse-drawn vehicles.

Opposite, bottom: Wilhelm, Hattie, family members and bakers in front of the Liberty and Dudley Street store.

The ultra-modern bakeshop of 1906. I'll bet it was hot in there.

Bakery opened to the public at 7:00 a.m. As shared with columnist Willard Clopton for a 1961 *Post Time Star* article, Hattie explained that during this era, "Bakeries used to be mostly in cellars" and "most all of what we sold was handmade." Owning and operating an electric vertical mixer in their early years (most likely by 1915) was almost extravagant and definitely state-of-the-art technology.

On the day before Mother's Day in 1919, William was shot and murdered in a robbery near his home on Epworth Avenue in Westwood. His teenage sons, Bill and Carl, witnessed the holdup and ran away. One of the attackers, who had previously been employed by William, knew that the bakery would have been busy that day and assumed William was carrying the day's profits, when in fact he only had twenty-seven dollars. The man who shot him was sentenced to death.

Hattie continued to own and run the bakery, initially with the help of both of her sons. Several years later, Bill left the bakery business in order to go to college and then pursue his own bakery venture. Carl stayed with Hattie, and the downtown bakery was in operation until the Great Flood of 1937, when the Ohio River crested at eighty feet and inundated the shop. As shared with Mr. Clopton, floodwater "filled up the cellar. Bread and rolls

Look at the size of that coal-fired oven. Notice the peel sticks hanging from the rack in the upper right of the photo.

floated all over town." By that time, Bill had owned and operated Virginia Bakery for ten years. Hattie and Carl ended up joining the team in Clifton, where she worked in the retail shop as a counter lady.

Carl worked in the "front shop" (the bakers' room most easily seen by the customers) of the two back sections, the area where the cakes, pies and delicate pastries were made. Carl was described by some of the men who worked with him as "kind of quiet" and "really good at cakes and pies." He was precise in measurements, and having so much experience, he was very accurate by sight. He also watched everything carefully so the quality of the baked goods was always consistent. His son, Dick, quotes Carl as saying, "'Once you start messing with the food business, people know it right away.' He would never use anything but whole eggs, sugar, flour—everything was original." Carl's wife, Lydia, also worked at the bakery and would come in on Fridays and sometimes on Saturdays, bringing him a meal to make sure he got something to eat on those days when he worked late.

By the 1950s, Hattie had seen a change in the shopping style of bakery customers. Fridays and Saturdays were the busiest days, with women coming by car and buying enough items to stock up. Many bought a variety of eight

Left: Bill and Carl Thie as young boys.

Below: Hattie with her teenage sons, Carl and Bill. I believe this photo was taken shortly after my great-grandfather was shot in a holdup.

And approximately forty years later, Bill, Hattie and Carl still made up the "Thie Team." *Courtesy of the General Mills Archives.*

to ten items and then wrapped and froze several of the baked goods to keep them fresh throughout the week.

After moving up to Clifton, "Grandma Thie," as Hattie was called by both family and customers, lived in an apartment above the bakery and was an integral part of the operation. Still on the job every day working as hard as the younger folks when she was in her seventies, Paddleford described her as a "small angular woman with…gray hair and blue-gray eyes" who loved to greet all the customers, asking about family members if she knew them well. Others remember her as a little woman full of spit and fire, with a sense of humor. In her interview with Mr. Clopton at the age of eighty, she joked, "And I've never yet scorched a lady finger—except my own, now and then."

Although her sons had been encouraging her to retire when she was in her early seventies, she had merely been amused by the idea and had had no interest in doing so. "Retire? Me? It's never entered my mind." She felt her catnaps kept her going, and she knew if she were to retire she wouldn't get to see her family as much or all the customers she had become friends with over the years. They all meant a great deal to her. "Baking is more than making dough, you know," she told Mr. Clopton. She was proud that the family—her two sons, Bill and Carl, and two of her grandsons, Howard and Paul, who were just beginning to get into the bakery business—all worked together. Even years later, people commented on how spry Grandma Thie was as she continued to work in the bakery. At eighty years of age, she still answered the phone and handled other light duties—such as the fruit preparation of peeling peaches, breaking plums in half and taking the seeds out—so that she could provide service and be part of the action. Jenny Thie, Hattie's great-granddaughter, reported that Hattie was the most frugal of all the Thies, which she laughingly added was saying a lot. She loved to tell stories of growing up in Germany and the hardships she faced as a young girl.

During the time Hattie lived above the bakery, her daughter-in-law, Myrtle, always made dinner for her, and Hattie would often give the meal away to someone else. As also shared by Jenny, Myrtle would ask, "Mom, how did you like the stew?" "Oh, I don't know; I gave it to Hermie Lee [Jackson] and I had whipped cream pie." The interchange appeared to be their way of needling each other. From appearances, Grandma Thie didn't want her daughter-in-law to be one up on her because she was, after all, the matriarch of the whole place. She possessed and wielded the power to make things either go smoothly or not.

SECOND GENERATION OF THE THIE BAKERY FAMILY IN CINCINNATI

In the years immediately following his father's murder, William F. "Bill" Thie continued his schooling and met Myrtle. Bill used to tell the story that in ninth grade, while waiting for the bus that went from Westwood to Clifton, he looked across the street and told his friend, "See that girl over there? I'm going to marry her one day!" Bill graduated from Hughes High School, as did Myrtle. Bill then went to the seminary for a while, missed Myrtle and returned home, attended the University of Cincinnati (along with Myrtle) for two years and then spent one year at law school. In 1925, Bill and Myrtle were married, and one year later their first son, William Howard, was born. In the following years, five more children came along: Paul, Ronald, Janet, Sandra and Sharon.

After spending some time selling bakery supplies and working at another bakery in Mariemont for about a year, Bill decided he wanted to establish and run his own retail baking business. In 1927, he made the decision to accept a loan for $2,400 (quite a large amount in 1927) from his father-in-law in order to purchase the now landmark building on Ludlow Avenue, which included the retail shop, from Virginia May. Dick remembers being told that the original store was named Virginia's Pastry Shop. When Bill took over, he chose to use a similar name to encourage former customers to keep

Bill standing near cash register in the Mariemont bakery where he worked for a brief time.

coming back. The bill of sale included two small bake ovens, one J.H. Day dough mixer, one Triumph cake machine, two shop tables, one workbench, one stove, one flour container, any and all tools, the cash register, store fixtures, an icebox, wall cases, linoleum on the floor and all paper stock in the store. For Bill, borrowing the money from Louis Suhre was one of the hardest things he ever did and a huge personal embarrassment. Because of this uncomfortable indebtedness, he worked very hard to pay back the entire loan quickly. Starting with his first day's profit of $26.86 (for 154 items sold) and with receipts continuing upward, Bill made his final payment during the first year of operation.

Virginia Bakery opened on April 18, 1927, under the new management. According to George Chussler in the Associated Retail Bakers of America (ARBA) November 1961 newsletter, over time Virginia Bakery became "recognized as one of the country's finest retail establishments." Bill was proud of being a retail baker, and this attitude came across to both his employees and his customers. Many of the bakers who worked in the shop were attracted to and mentioned Bill's personality, his work ethic and his sense of values. He was the first person in the bakery in the morning, usually starting his day by 5:00 a.m., while other bakers didn't show up until about 6:00 a.m. He was a very strong figure, "The Boss" who held down the place.

The bakery was Bill's world, and he had his own unique way of relating to people. While he had a relaxed way about him, he was an extremely strict taskmaster. He followed an inflexible routine, and as Bill Pritz (a former young employee) shared, "If you varied from it, he wouldn't even say anything—he'd just grab you and point you in the direction you were supposed to go. There was no real instruction, he'd just sort of push you along your way and you'd figure out what you were supposed to do. He seemed like the last generation of that kind of person—something to emulate—a standard to measure myself by."

Mr. Chussler wrote that among his friends and colleagues, "those who know him best, [Bill] is beloved for his modesty and sincerity and for his keen wit and humor which have earned for him the respect and affection of his fellow bakers and the reference to him as the 'Will Rogers' of the baking industry." He was "looked upon for leadership because of his great faith—his faith in God, his faith in fellow man and his unflinching faith in the future of retail baking."

Bill had a history of being an involved, active member of the organizations he joined. He was one of the original members of the local Cincinnati Retail Bakers Association and in 1941 was president. Years later, he held the title again when the organization was renamed the Greater Cincinnati Retail Bakers Association (GCRBA) because of its broader base. Under his administrative leadership, he created promotions such as Mother's Day Mothers and Retail Bakers Night at the Ball Park (the Reds' old Crosley Field), where cakes were presented to the players.

Over a period of many years, Bill filled positions as director, a member of the executive committee and treasurer of the ARBA. In 1953, Bill was elected president of the National Retail Bakers Association and served two terms, getting to know people from all locales. As such, Richard Gordon wrote in his 1954 article for the *Cincinnati Post* that "in a sense, he is the head baker in the country." In a 1960 *Vitality News*, the Merchandising Feature columnist interviewed Bill. "That Bill Thie takes very seriously his work to meet and discuss with bakers [the opportunities] of mutual benefit [provided by the ARBA] is proven by the fact that in the past six years he has visited bakers and bakery associations in 40 states." In the 1961 monthly article, Mr. Chussler wrote that Bill was known across the country, via his appearances at conventions and meeting programs, for his breadth of knowledge and sound counsel concerning issues bakers faced. "Bill captivated his audience with his down to earth logic and sound reasoning to the point that [at one convention] he 'stole the show' and this was acknowledged by the [key speaker] who followed him and who was an accomplished performer and chosen for this reason." Bill was also involved with the Ohio Bakers Association, and by 1961 he was serving as the vice-president. With this group, as with the others, he "in every instance contributed unselfishly for the benefit of his fellow retail bakers."

Earl Kramer, the former owner of Cincinnati Bakers Supply Company, "knew good old Bill pretty darn well," dirty glasses and all. (Bill was always fidgeting while he was doing this and that, and his glasses were always smeared with butter and flour and a little bit of everything else.) Earl knew Bill to be a fine gentleman, a straight shooter, a good man who raised a good family. "He was a hard worker—there's no question about that—and he had one heck of a business head." Merchandising, selling phases and production were all areas that Bill studied with shrewd perception.

In one circumstance, his desire for a better product actually led to the creation of another man's business. The effects of the Great Depression were still present in 1932, when Omer Smith was happy to get employment with a paper distributor, calling on bakers and providing the supplies they needed. On one of his visits to Virginia Bakery, Bill asked him for white-lined corrugated cake servers—they had brown ones, but Bill wanted white ones for a nicer presentation of the cakes. The paper company did not make white ones and had no plans to do so. Omer decided to take the matter into his own hands, ingeniously designed a way to make some at home and ended up selling his white-lined corrugated cake circles to virtually every retail bakery in Cincinnati as a result of Bill's original vision.

Bakers in 1932. I loved that oven they're standing next to. It blew up in 1983. Fortunately, we were closed for vacation, so there were no injuries.

Ron Thie, Bill's third son, did not inherit the love of the bakery business as his older brothers Howard and Paul did. He remembers the time when he was in college and his father was president of the ARBA. Bill wanted Ron to come home so that he could attend the annual convention, which was held in Cincinnati that particular year. Bill wanted Ron to hear him give his talks, one of which was titled "I Want My Sons To Be Bakers." Ron's reaction, knowing the hard work and long, unusual hours of physical labor involved with the profession, was, "That man is sick." Bill's second speech, or "harangue" as Ron lovingly teases, was about the importance of not cheating on the quality of ingredients. In 1960, he continued to spread that message to other bakers in his interview with *Vitality News*. "Convenience without quality is useless. You still have to turn out a quality product in good variety to keep them coming back…Sometimes the temptation may be great to substitute on ingredients—to cut down on quality, but this is false economy…you are shortchanging only yourself." Bill's son, Howard, and grandson, Tom, later carried on the tradition of "refusing to settle for any ingredients less than the best." Deborah Rieselman went on to say in her *Clifton Living* newspaper article that "some say Thie uses more real butter and fresh cream than all the other bakeries in town combined."

When asked by columnist Polk Laffoon IV for the *Cincinnati Post* in 1977 what the secret of his business success was, Bill's immediate answer was "quality." He always made sure the products Virginia Bakery used were top notch and knew that doing so paid off.

Bill's daughter, Janet, clearly remembers an afternoon when she was entering the bakery after school. There was a margarine salesman coming out of the back door, while another salesman was approaching to go in. The first one said to the second one, "I hope you're not trying to sell margarine because you won't sell any here." Janet went in and said, "Daddy, that guy is really mad," to which Bill said, "Well, I just don't believe in it."

In general, Bill loved to see the salesmen show up at the bakery in their dark suits. He would dip his hand in the flour barrel when they weren't looking, give them a hearty slap on the back and wish them a wonderful day as they left…and then laugh out loud with the bakers when they were out of earshot.

The following story demonstrates how, on occasion, Bill entered gray areas of ethical behavior but also underscores his strong belief in using quality products. Ron agreed to share the tale because the parties involved have passed away and enough time has gone by so that no one will be sent to jail. During World War II, sugar was rationed. Each time the man who sold Bill sugar at that time would come in the bakery, he'd say, "This rationing is ridiculous. We have a warehouse full of sugar, but we can't sell it. There are barges sitting down on the Ohio River right now filled with sugar that we can't even unload because the warehouse is too full." Provoked and inspired, Bill hatched a plan. His son, Paul, and a man who ran the gas station behind the bakery would go down to the landing in the dark of night and back a pickup truck onto the barge. They handed the guard standing there a twenty-dollar bill. After spreading a clean canvas tarp in the bed of the pickup, they shoveled away, filling the back with this contraband substance.

Journaling played an important role in properly managing the bakery operation. *The Day-by-Day Book for Retail Bakers* from 1927–28 provides a great deal of insight about Bill and Myrtle's first year of owning Virginia Bakery. (Identical books were used by Howard and Tom throughout the years.) The notes he made provided important information about bookkeeping on a daily basis, which by year's end provided legal sales records and basic costs history of the business. Remarks were noted about the weather, as sales were impacted if it rained all day or was extremely hot; about particular products: the day's best seller, too much of one type of cake being made, which created too many leftover items, or not enough of a certain item being baked, as

The interior photo taken in 1932 is the earliest picture we have of Virginia Bakery's front retail shop.

expressed in "not enough yeast goods"; about a church or some other group having placed an order; about holidays and staying open later than usual; and about positive updates, such as "Best Monday yet."

While Bill worked the back shop, he was also known for popping out front (likely covered with a coating of flour) to offer customers a taste of different items. He was proud of his baked goods, especially his hard rolls, and would hand them out warm with slabs of butter on top as he said, "Taste this; it's so good." On one occasion, Bill was observed handing out a roll to someone who had been in the bakery the day before. When she said, "I had one yesterday," he handed her the new roll and said, "They're better today."

Bill was a kind and generous man. In one instance during World War II, Joe Arnult, one of his back shop workers, was called into the navy. In order to save this spot, Bill hired his younger brother Ed (still in the eighth grade) after Ed convinced Bill that he was a diligent and fast worker. In another, Berthold Schwegmann emigrated from Germany in the hopes of opening his own bakery one day. Bill hired him, and although Berthold had already been a baker, he felt he learned a great deal at Virginia Bakery (which he later took with him for his own enterprise), and a long-lasting relationship was formed.

Bill's willingness to help others also freed him of a previously established pattern. In the late nineteenth century and into the twentieth, there were a very large number of successful bakeries established in the downtown area that were physically very close together. For example, around Liberty Street where his parents had their bakery, there were individual blocks that held multiple bakeries, some literally almost touching one another. In those days, the bakery families were very protective of their space, afraid that family recipe secrets would be stolen. If, for example, a baker went out back and saw his son playing with another baker's son, he would run him off; and the other father would have done the same. And if a baker worked for one company, everybody knew "You work for them," and he would not ever be hired to work at one of the other bakeries, a trend that actually continued into modern times. While Bill still kept his recipes to himself, he did extend friendship and help to other bakers, sometimes offering advice to those just beginning, as he did with Bill Hartman when he started his own bakery in Price Hill, and at other times offering sympathy for a grieving colleague's family by providing baked goods for the wake, as he did for the Hess family.

Despite keeping such uncommon hours, Bill definitely enjoyed a social life. He enjoyed going to Mecklenburg's Garden restaurant immensely. He undoubtedly loved the authentic German atmosphere with the grapevine-trellised outdoor beer garden and eating area, good ethnic food and the camaraderie of playing pinochle with his buddies.

Bill and Myrtle were also known for throwing huge annual bakers' picnics in the summertime at their twenty-two-acre farm on Hanley Road. The picnics were always preceded by planning sessions a couple weeks in advance of the big events, which also were filled with good food, a brief meeting and fun and games. Myrtle and other family members did all the cooking for these gatherings. Among the menu items provided was Grandma Suhre's ("tons and tons of") sweet sour slaw. The guest list was made up of members of the GCRBA, also referred to as Allied Members, which was composed of bakers and the retail salesmen/suppliers who sold them flour, sugar and other bakery products. At least one hundred people would attend and enjoy the homemade food and beer (the beverage of choice among all the bakers), play cards (poker and pinochle) and participate in the ball game between the bakers and the salesmen/suppliers. The softball games were always very competitive and incited many arguments about foul balls and whether a player was safe or out. However, whether the Thies knew or not, the Allieds were smart enough to always let the Bakers win the games in the end, according to Mary Ann Acree, secretary for the GCRBA and the

Howard and Paul, the baking brothers.

wife of one of the bakers. "After all, they were the customers!" Other events were offered as well, like Bill selling three chances at hitting a golf ball into the pond. Ron thinks he charged one dollar and if someone hit a ball in the pond he'd win ten dollars, but he doesn't remember anyone ever succeeding.

At other events, entire families were invited. Their grandson Tom was very young when he attended, maybe four or five years old, but he remembers a lot of people and children. The kids were not supposed to go near the shelter house, because that's where the men played pinochle and drank their beer. For a treat, they could take their little bottles of Coke to his grandfather, Bill, and he would "open them with his teeth." Actually, he would turn so they couldn't see and use a bottle opener. Then he would steal their noses, using the old thumb between the finger trick, and make them beg for their noses back. Good times. German humor!

Bill and Myrtle produced what many would have called a perfect household. As described by George Amick in an article for the *Cincinnati Enquirer* in 1956, "The family used to have a garden, chickens and cows for the growing youngsters to care for, but that was abandoned as they got married and moved out on their own." The Thies were actually entered into a contest by an undisclosed friend and were "in the running for 'All American Family'…a nationwide contest sponsored by the Boys Clubs of America and the Grolier Society, publishers of *The Book of Knowledge*." Bill and Myrtle also had a place in Michigan, on Torch Lake, where they, their family and friends (including some of the bakery's employees) summered together—visiting, relaxing and enjoying one another's company. From the time they married until their deaths, they vacationed every summer at Torch Lake. Mr. Amick pointed out that "the family's fondness for doing things together is shown by the annual summer 'caravan'…where one cabin houses the whole three-generation group." Bill had grown up spending his summers in that area, going to Camp Fairwood as a young boy and then as a counselor, teaching horseback riding. The couple even went there on their honeymoon, and Myrtle spent part of her time darning socks for the campers. After years of renting cabins, they bought property and built a cottage in 1938. Bill loved Torch Lake because the area was cool and

Through the years, the time spent at Torch Lake provided a wonderful change of pace. Fishing was practically mandatory, as were the family costume parties, which added to the fun.

beautiful, a great change from the hot bakery. And while he was known for being a character in general, he seemed to let loose a little more when up at the lake, as expressed by his love of wearing costumes while there. He and his brother Carl would divide up the summer so that each of them could get some time away from the bakery.

There was a time when Bill and his sons, Howard, Paul and Ron, took their trade with them while on vacation. They would go and bake very early in the morning at a storefront in Bellaire, Michigan, and then the lady who lived in the house would sell the baked goods. After the work was done, Bill and his boys would go back to the cottage and go fishing and sailing or spend their time in some other fun way.

In 1977, the Thies' Virginia Bakery celebrated its fiftieth anniversary. Bill was seventy-three years old and still full of life and quite active, finding delight in just about everything. At that age, he still went in to work about 5:00 a.m. in order to set and mix the dough for the bakers who came in after him, and he would remain in the back working until late afternoon. Polk Laffoon observed, as he interviewed Bill for the event, "He opens ovens, shovels sugar, lifts lard…In his black work shoes, white suit, white apron and white cap, he almost seems to be made from flour himself…Thie is an old-school craftsman who probably can't imagine not working six days a week and probably only regards it a matter of passing interest that his business reached the half century mark…his mother worked until she died in 1963, and you understand that, for him, that's the way things are."

On the day of the bakery's anniversary, the front shop was filled with flowers and congratulations. Bill received an award plaque and recognition from the GCRBA for being in business for fifty years, and someone gave him a little hat with "50" on it that he walked around wearing for the day. Myrtle's idea was to give him a hoagie with "50" written on it, which he called "a woman's idea."

While the comment above may sound a little macho, Bill held his wife in high esteem, as is clearly evident in a passage he wrote in his personal journal on July 2, 1972: "6:00 AM—Good night's sleep—47th wedding anniversary—Thanks be to God for blessing my life with Myrtle. I could never live long enough to give her all the love and attention she so richly deserves."

Myrtle was a very outgoing, peppy lady and a true partner in all areas of their life. In the fifty-three years that Bill and Myrtle were married, they built a loving family and a strong, successful business together. Myrtle had a lot on her plate. In addition to working at the bakery in the front of the store,

I absolutely love this picture. Bill holding Sharon, Paul, Ron, Janet, Howard, Myrtle holding Sandra. The living room on Hanley Road. *Photographed by Childs.*

she took care of their six children and kept things at home in order. If that wasn't enough, she did all the bookkeeping for the bakery, often tackling the managerial matters and payrolls after the children were in bed, staying up until 2:00 a.m., almost about the time Bill would be getting up to start his day and head for the bakery. Myrtle also was in charge of creating pleasing window displays and won many awards for her decorating efforts. Before the bakery was remodeled in the 1950s, there were two display windows. She would change the decorations depending on the season or depending on what events were happening in Cincinnati.

Being on "opposite" schedules, Bill and Myrtle would sometimes wave to each other as they passed on Colerain Avenue, he headed home and she on her way to the bakery. Whereas he went in early to start the dough, she'd go in the afternoon in order to be there to close the store. Before leaving home, Myrtle would prepare a meal and have supper simmering for Bill when he'd get there (the same meal she had packed for Hattie). Many times, especially around the holidays, she'd also cook for all the bakery employees.

Myrtle and Bill definitely developed a schedule that most would consider unusual, but that worked for them. On their fiftieth wedding anniversary, they joked that they had never thought of divorce because they never saw each other.

After the bakery's operation was handed over to their son, Howard, in 1976, Myrtle still went to the store to take care of the books. She helped with the transition as best she could. So without hard feelings, she felt it was time for Howard and Cindy to take over and for her to step down. When she retired at the age of seventy-four, she felt the time was right, but she really missed the customers.

As Bill had been, Myrtle was also a giving person. She taught Sunday school, was active in the women's association and played the piano and organ at the Westwood United Methodist Church. She also gave her time and talent to the St. Elizabeth Guild, for which she knitted hundreds of caps and booties for premature babies. Her daughter, Janet, remembers her as "a dream," adding, "Her little legs carried her many inches, that's for sure."

THIRD GENERATION OF THE THIE BAKERY FAMILY IN CINCINNATI

Howard Thie grew up in the Westwood and White Oak areas of Cincinnati and went to Colerain High School. A member of the class of 1944, he was known as "Red Thie" because of the color of his hair. Being one of Bill and Myrtle's children, he spent a lot of time in the bakery and learned the secrets of the baking trade from his father, who passed down his knowledge, secrets and techniques. Starting out in the bakery business as a young man, Howard also worked with his uncle on the front bench (table), where Carl taught him the duties of the front shop: cakes, pastries and pies.

Not long after graduation, in 1945, Howard entered the navy and spent time in the Pacific Theater. Howard wanted to serve his country in the worst way and finally was enlisted after his third attempt at boot camp; he had difficulty enlisting due to his flat feet and asthma. His duty as a baker was onboard an LST (landing ship tank) headed for Okinawa. The ship became stranded on a reef for a week. During this time, the Japanese surrendered, and the crew on board had to wait for a tow home. The family has always found this story of Howard's great, illustrious naval career to be amusing. From his experience, Howard shared with Tom that working on a constantly

Bill and Myrtle's family several years later in front of the Hanley Road home. *Courtesy of the Gilbert H. Corlett family, Gil Corlett Photography.*

rocking ship, swaying back and forth, was the most difficult baking challenge he'd ever encountered.

Once safely back home, with the war behind him, Howard joined the bakery's crew full time. Along with his father, he put in long days dealing with heavy containers and trays and very hot ovens from which occasional breaks were needed. Howard would go outside on the back steps to cool off and get a bit of fresh air during these interruptions from work. He oftentimes observed a girl walking down Hosea Avenue and then crossing through the parking lot to Ludlow. He noticed a pattern of when this cute girl would pass by and made an effort to take his breaks accordingly. Family stories tell that Howard might have made some catcalls, but they know for certain that he offered free baked goods. With some persistence, "Hey, you want a doughnut?" turned out to be his successful pickup line. As reported with a laugh by their daughter, Jenny, at some point Cindy gave in, "for doughnuts more than anything." Tom remembers her saying, "He was the ugliest redhead I ever saw, but those doughnuts smelled great!"

Cordelia "Cindy" Leathers was born in Central City, Kentucky, and grew up in a very close family who had to do everything for themselves during the Great Depression. When her mother remarried in 1935, they all moved to Verona, Kentucky.

After graduating from the Walton-Verona High School, her older sister, Dorothy, asked her what she planned on doing with her life. Cindy replied that she hadn't decided, but she mentioned that she had thought about being a nurse. Immediately following that conversation, Cindy arranged a trip that involved a stopover at Dorothy's in Lawrenceburg, Indiana, a ride for both of them on the Southeastern Bus line to downtown Cincinnati, followed by a transfer to a streetcar that dropped them off right in front of Good Samaritan Hospital on Clifton Avenue. The two sisters felt God was with them as they were ushered into the director of nursing's office and introduced themselves. Although all the classes were filled that day, in less than two weeks, Cindy received a call saying someone had dropped out and she could start soon. She felt a miracle had happened when they told her the class she would be joining was the last nursing program that the U.S. Navy was paying for because the war was ending.

In 1945, Cindy graduated with honors from Good Sam as a registered nurse. She, along with two other nurses who continued their work at Good Sam, rented an apartment that was close to Virginia Bakery. The story of how Cindy and Howard met and started going out, as told by the Leathers family, is similar to the Thies' version and testifies to the mutual attraction. As Cindy carried her textbooks to and from classes, she walked through Virginia Bakery's parking lot. "Glancing through the side window, over the big table where Howard kneaded the bread dough, Cindy made eye contact with the young, freckle-faced redhead. Of course, she had to go inside the store for some snacks, and of course, Howard, the proverbial host, came to greet her. The rest is history."

The couple married in 1950, and Howard baked and decorated the cake, which was a large, three-layered masterpiece designed to look like the church's interior. The bride and groom figurines led the procession, while the bridesmaids (dressed in outfits that were color matched to the actual chiffon pastel southern garden dresses and big brimmed hats worn by Cindy's attendants) marched down the aisle. Over the next eight years, they had three children: Jennifer, Deborah and Thomas.

Their first apartment was on Glendora Avenue in Clifton, followed by a home on Banning Road until they outgrew the space. They eventually built

To Cindy, with Love, Howard. The cake he made for their wedding.

a house in White Oak on Weiss Road (home of the raspberry patch and apple orchard that provided some fruit used in the baked goods) near where Bill and Myrtle lived.

After Carl had a heart attack at the bakery and died in 1967, Howard took over the front shop. Over the years, Howard gained a great deal of the experience that helped him eventually become a Certified Master Baker—one of the first group of seven in the United States in the mid-1990s. Annie Glenn, one of the shop girls who liked watching Howard work, remembers him using his bare hands to top the lemon meringue pies. "He wanted his baked goods to come out just right!" For many years as the cake decorator, Howard was in charge of making special occasion cakes and the wedding cakes, where he proved his skills and abilities. "In addition to creating special memories for countless weddings," Rebecca Billman pointed out in her December 1999 piece for the *Cincinnati Enquirer*, "he decorated cakes for Reds celebrations and" for other commemorative events. His son Tom added, "Everything he made, he made well."

Batter up! Howard hits a home run with the Reds at Crosley Field. *Photographed by Howard Pille.*

Howard had worked at the bakery for over forty years when, in 1976, he and Cindy bought the family business from his father Bill, and he remained in charge for approximately the next twenty years. Shortly after he took over the operation, Cindy retired from her job as a nurse and started working at the bakery. Cindy helped by managing the bakery. She was very determined and had her own ideas of how things should be done—and they weren't anything like the old way, the way Myrtle had managed things for Bill. To Myrtle, Cindy quite possibly looked like a young whippersnapper trying to take over things. Whatever her thoughts or feelings about family politics, this was the period of time when Myrtle graciously chose to retire.

Howard had also learned a secret about juggling his career and home life. In an article by Deborah Rieselman for *Clifton Living* in the early 1980s, she wrote, "Most bakers get used to two things: sleeping alone and watching the sunrise every morning. Traditionally, bakers work straight through the middle of the night." Howard, however, learned the trick for "having happier customers and a less-lonely wife. The owner of Virginia Bakery is probably the only baker in town who bakes exclusively during the day…When Thie says his customers get fresh-baked goods, he means fresh—so fresh that they are often still hot when purchased."

Although Cindy's training as a nurse had not prepared her for the job of cake decorator, her hobbies perhaps had. She had a natural artistic bent, which included painting, ceramics, macramé, upholstery, refinishing furniture, cooking and entertaining. Cindy was self taught and developed her own techniques and tools, which is probably why she was so successful. Rather than follow current standards, she set her own. She didn't know what

This is how I remember my dad at work. Content and humble. You wouldn't know he was a master baker.

was right or wrong; she just knew how to make the process work for each individual bride. Not much of a wedding cake business existed before her efforts; the wedding cakes had previously been more like big birthday cakes. For almost fifteen years, Cindy worked in a room above the bakery that was set up just for the purpose of decorating cakes. She loved the work and became quite a skilled, often imitated decorator, creating magnificent cakes and later even teaching others, including her daughter-in-law, Moe. During the wedding season, May and June, she had to set a limit of making ten cakes per week. Turning down 150 brides-to-be during those two months was not uncommon for Cindy. Because she decorated the cakes herself and was unable to decorate any more than her limit, Cindy did not represent Virginia bakery at bridal shows.

During the fall of each year in the early and mid-1980s, competitions were held for bakers at Northgate and Tri-County Malls. For these, Cindy would have the bakers bake certain items that Virginia Bakery was really good at and known for, such as a display of cakes; French bread and other breads; schnecken; brownies; and even a wedding cake. She and one of the bakers, often Jerry Armstead, would go out and set them up ("adding a nice shiny sugar glaze when appropriate") alongside all the other retail bakers.

Another master at work. Cindy starting a wedding cake. Some took twelve to fifteen hours.

As a member of the GCRBA, Cindy gave demonstrations at some of the seminar workshops. At both local and national events, the bakers created a bakery right in center of the convention floor, and Cindy taught programs on how to make a wedding cake.

Howard, like his father, was very active with the retail bakers' associations and twice held the position of president of the Greater Cincinnati Retail Bakers Association, as well as being on the board of directors. Virginia Bakery always participated in the promotions of the Cincinnati bakers, such as giving out cupcakes on Fountain Square and sponsoring a child for the nationwide Little Miss Muffin contest, National Retail Bakers Week and the Cincinnati Bicentennial Celebration. Bill Hartman, owner of the St. Lawrence Bakery, met and got to know Howard well in the early 1950s when they started the Young Bakers Club. Their intended goal was to get young people interested in working in the bakery profession. The plan worked for a while but then became more difficult—mostly because the younger generation was not interested in working the necessary hours.

The family characteristics of being kind, friendly, generous people were passed down via Howard and Cindy. Many customers commented

The Northgate show around 1985. My mom loved to show off. She was a proud woman, deservedly.

on the fact that the Thies were good, nice people. They loved the fact that Howard would oftentimes come out front and say hello or, if too busy for that, at least always acknowledge that you were in the store with a nod, a smile or a wave. From various reports, Clifton retailers knew everyone in the bakery and considered the Thies to be great people, and great teases, who certainly loved their work. Many of the neighborhood business owners purportedly had a back-door policy. They popped in to visit Howard and his brother Paul in the late afternoon and left with a bag full of goodies.

Howard was not as flamboyant as his father Bill, but he too had a great sense of humor. In the 1970s when "streakers" were capturing national attention, Howard made a huge sign and put it in the front window: "FREE DOUGHNUTS FOR STREAKERS." Tom remembers his father as a devout family man who would work six days a week and still attend every one of his children's baseball games, scout meetings and piano recitals. Others, according to George Amick's 1956 *Cincinnati Enquirer* article, remember Howard as being "named unofficial 'social chairman' for canasta parties." Sunday was his day to cook, starting with a huge breakfast and ending with

Cindy and Howard at home on Weiss Road.

a scrumptious dinner, usually a one-pot dish like chili or stew. He also loved to grill. Tom thinks his family was his father's only hobby.

Howard, just like his father, loved his profession. In a 1980s interview with Deborah Rieselman, Cindy said she couldn't "imagine what Howard would do if he couldn't bake." Sharing his inherent love of cooking and baking extended beyond the family and business to the people and activities important to him and his family. Helen Adams, another student in Tom's piano class, shared that "the promise of Virginia Bakery treats waiting for me afterward took my mind off my pre-recital nerves. I felt like I was in the company of greatness on those occasions." Nieces and nephews shared their delight with such goodies also. Dennis Doggett wrote, "Every Christmas, Cindy and Howard would bring many white boxes with the red Virginia Bakery markings on it…This was in the days before diets, cholesterol warnings, etc. were drummed into our heads—this was simply heavenly enjoyment…it was a fun part of growing up." Beyond Clifton and family, during the summer of 1973, the Thies offered another type of generosity when they opened the doors of their place on Torch Lake to all the members of Tom's Boy Scout troop.

Strong ties were built with some of the employees as well; several employees regard the Thies as a second family. Kristine Kessler shared, "There was no other person like Howard Thie. He always made wonderful pastries and he was a great cook. Whenever I was there around lunchtime, he would cook us a meal; I attest to this day that he taught me how to cook. I make his chili and meatloaf any chance I can get. Howard was like another grandfather to me. He even gave me some of his old cameras when I was taking a photography class." Ed Arnult remembers how Cindy and Howard gave him some prepaid ballroom dance lessons. And baker Jerry Armstead used to go out to the house and visit with Howard after he retired.

Cindy held a high standard for herself and worked very hard to build and establish a large wedding cake business for the bakery. She could be tough on some of her workers while at the same time often acting motherly, pushing them and encouraging them if she saw potential in them. This same attitude applied when teaching her daughter-in-law how to decorate wedding cakes.

Baker Bill and sons standing on the sidewalk by the bakery's back door.

Toward the end of Cindy's life, knowing she had cancer, she found herself in a somewhat similar position with Moe as she had been in with Myrtle. One can imagine that she might have had mixed feelings to deal with as she prepared to hand over the fame and glory, the product of all her hard work, to her daughter-in-law, a novice in the trade. Balancing an awareness of her own illness with her desire to teach Moe all she could about decorating, in order to feel assured that Moe would be able to handle the job, must have been somewhat difficult.

Like the close connection between Howard and some of the employees, the same could be said about Cindy. Before dying, she asked longtime employee Willie Little to be one of her pallbearers. Virginia Bakery was more than a business; Virginia Bakery was a family.

A slow transition took place starting in 1993, the year Cindy died, when Tom took over the back shop operation and the bookkeeping. Howard did not fully retire until 1997.

Paul, Bill and Myrtle's second child, was born in 1927, attended the Dunwoody School of Baking in Minnesota and was an excellent baker. He, as Howard, was also a talented decorator. Paul was creative in non-baking matters also. He liked giving people nicknames, and he could fix anything, but usually in an unconventional way. He hated to throw things away and would always be repairing things using the odds and ends he'd saved.

Paul and his wife, Joyce, had three boys, Paul Jr., Mark and Jim, who all worked in the bakery at one time or another. When Paul reached a point in his life when illness prevented him from working at the bakery, he took care of his mother, and she took care of him in their final years. He died in July 2001.

As noted earlier, Ron Thie, Howard's youngest brother, did not take to the bakery business. When Tom first contacted him to let him know that he was going to be interviewed for this book, his comment was, "I hope she doesn't want to know anything about baking."

At the age of about ten or eleven, Ron began a regular Saturday morning regime of leaving home by 6:00 a.m. and going to work at the bakery. This routine continued all the way through high school. He worked in the back shop most of the time, scraping pans and icing coffee cakes, tea rings and breakfast rolls; then he would carry finished baked goods down to the retail shop and put them in the counter cases.

When Ron was in college, he'd come home on weekends, at that point mainly to deliver wedding cakes, a job that he liked better. He said,

> *For your information, I believe I was the only wedding cake deliverer for Virginia Bakery who never dropped or damaged a wedding cake—my only bakery claim to fame! On second thought, Mom kept a book of everyone who was ever on the payroll at the bakery, and my name wasn't in it. All of my siblings and relatives who worked there were in the book, but not me. Mom laughed when I asked her why I wasn't listed. She said maybe I didn't work hard enough! Oh well—my second bakery claim to fame.*

What Ron remembers most about working in the bakery shops were the four German bakers, whom he found to be very entertaining. They came from different parts of Germany and spoke in different dialects, and when he wasn't doing his work properly they all had a different name for him, such as "schlau meier" (smart mouthed) and "boser bub" (bad boy). He'd ask, "What does that mean?" and they all said basically the same thing—that he was a lazy boy. Other than hearing himself being badgered, Ron liked listening to them talk about the Fatherland. On one Saturday in 1950, he heard three things that he found quite interesting and that made quite an impression on the teenager: (1) One of the bakers had gone back to Germany, and all the rest of them were really excited to hear about the trip. Long story short, he told them they were lucky to be here in the United States. (2) Just like his grandmother, the bakers were always saying so many wonderful things about Germany. So Ron asked them why, when they were always talking about how much they loved their Fatherland, they came over here in the first place. The answer was to avoid taxes and the draft. (They had come over before World War II, during the time Kaiser Wilhelm ruled the country.) (3) Ron's mother, who did the paperwork and bookkeeping, handed a pay envelope to one of these men. On the outside was written gross, social security number, income tax, etc. The baker said, "How come this go down?" Myrtle's answer was because the taxes went up, to which he replied, "If this keep up, I move to Chicago."

I'll bet that guy in the suit had a white handprint on his back when he left. It was one of Bill's favorite tricks.

According to Ron, his parents didn't bring home very many bakery goods. Having one of his father's custard pies on a Wednesday night was a big treat. Saturday nights, they'd get a tea ring or a butter cake—whatever was left over at the end of the day. They would always bring home bread.

Although those of us who are Virginia Bakery fans simply can't fathom the phenomenon, while working there Ron grew to hate cookies. After standing there on a Sunday afternoon packing dozens after dozens of boxes, he came to dislike them. He hated fruitcakes for another reason: between Thanksgiving and Christmas, the family all sat around the kitchen table at home with crates of dates to cut following a very specific method. Each date was to be sliced down the length of the fruit and then cut across twice, making six pieces. His dad was against the idea of leaving the fruit whole because "That ruins the fruitcake." After doing this work, in Ron's opinion there was no such thing as a good fruitcake. Ron always wondered how his parents could enjoy Christmas because they were so busy working right up until the last minute.

⟫⟨

Janet, Myrtle and Bill's first daughter, was six years old when her mother put her up on a stepstool and taught her how to press down the register buttons and ring up twenty-five cents. At the time, Janet didn't want to be doing that, but she came to find that the job really helped her in math. Janet worked in the bakery through her high school years, by which point she was making sixty cents per hour. She thought this was wonderful; she could go next door to Stier's pharmacy and buy a chocolate soda at the counter. She continued to work there off and on until she was about twenty-one years old and starting her own family. Working at the bakery was expected, just part of being Thie children, and an experience she now acknowledges provided a great education for life in general.

She and her siblings either made boxes, stocked the shelves, swept, cleaned or whatever else they were told to do. About 1974, Janet went back and worked for another eight years, many of those years ones when Howard and Cindy ran the bakery. "That was fun getting back into it and seeing all the people that I'd made friends with over the years. You know, customers become part of your family. We worked hard, but it was a fun time…good memories." With the exception of the holidays. Echoing Ron's comments, "Christmas time was no fun. Christmas fruitcakes…" Janet reiterated the story of how they'd sit at home and have to cut up fruit with scissors until she and the others had blisters.

In response to the question about what her favorite items were, Janet shared that she had just recently told her husband, "I would give my right hand for one of the buttercream pockets…or an apricot or cheese. And their bran muffins couldn't be touched…oh, those were wonderful…and the butterscotch gems…we sold dozens and dozens and dozens of those. I can't pick out one favorite thing. Everything was good. You're making me hungry talking about all this."

⟫⟨

"Hard work" was what first came to mind when Sandra, the second daughter and fifth child, was asked to share her thoughts about Virginia Bakery. "It was a family enterprise; you knew you were expected to be a part of that. All six of us worked there at some point—at various times and in different parts of the bakery. Brothers were mostly in the back shops where the baking took place, girls usually in the front selling…so many years, so much a part of our lives." The children always worked on Saturdays (from the time the bakery opened in the morning until anytime from 4:00 to as late as 7:00 p.m.) and whenever they were needed during the holidays because things were so busy. During their high school years, because the bakery was on the way home from Walnut Hills to White Oak, they would often help wait on customers for a couple of hours after school until their father was ready to take them home. Sandra continued to work through college, and then she came back even after she was married to help out during peak times.

Once again, the subject of labor involved with Christmas fruitcakes was brought to light. Cutting the various fruits that their father brought home into little pieces for the cake recipe was the priority—the job to be tackled even before homework. There were many long nights spent so that everything was properly prepared for the next morning.

Like other family members, Sandra can still remember certain families' standing orders. She can also remember when butterscotch gems were forty-eight cents a dozen and bread was sixteen cents for a small homemade and eighteen for a large.

Sandra respects what her father did, that he was so hardworking and how well he provided for his family. "We had it all available…very spoiled. The only thing we didn't have were boxes of cereal at home," she added with a laugh, well aware that most of us would have gladly exchanged our cereal for a good baked item any morning.

⋙⋙◆⋘⋘

Sharon, Bill and Myrtle's youngest child, did not have a strong interest in the bakery and ended up not working there as much as the other children, but she did go in on Sundays to help with the baking of cookies between Thanksgiving and Christmas. Those times would go on all afternoon and into the evening. Her normally assigned job was to clean the house and work at home.

When she was a little girl, Sharon loved horses and had a pony on the Hanley Road property. She had curly red hair, which made her look like a little Shirley Temple. She loved the theater, and when she was a junior at Walnut Hills High School, she wrote a play for the *Peanuts* yearly variety show. After graduating from there, she attended Mount Holyoke College and then settled in New York City, not coming home very often. Sharon was a writer and taught creative writing at the New School. She also worked in the advertising department of the *American Journal of Nursing* at one time. Sharon died in 1989.

FOURTH GENERATION OF THE THIE BAKERY FAMILY IN CINCINNATI

Jenny was the firstborn child of Howard and Cindy. The majority of her formative years involved the bakery. As with previous generations, she worked there while in high school and during her first two years of college and lived over the bakery when she went to the University of Cincinnati. When she transferred to Boston University and then went to medical school at UC, she didn't have the time to work in the bakery anymore, but she loved the time she'd been there. "There was a real cast of characters both behind and in front of the counter." She enjoyed meeting and interacting with the customers, getting to really know the people. As a proven pattern over the decades, "They'd come in and get the same thing most of the time—their standing orders."

Besides working with the whole family, Jenny recalls that being around the older counter ladies who worked there regularly was quite interesting: "They were a trip." While for the most part the staff was very friendly and accommodating, some of the older ladies were known for being a bit gruff and unfriendly at times. Jenny also remembers the old German bakers, some of whom still spoke German (in the 1960s) as they all worked in the back making the delicious baked goods.

Among Jenny's favorite items were her father's chocolate cream pies with a chocolate custard pudding and whipped cream, éclairs with custard cream and the custard puffs that didn't have chocolate on them, as well as the Christmas cookies. She loved the variety.

Other fond memories include attending her grandparents' big picnics, where all the card tables and lights set up created an atmosphere of fun and anticipation. As a child, she and others would love to go because they knew after an evening of the older folks drinking beer, playing cards and dropping some of their gambling money without being aware of doing so, the next morning they'd be able to scour the area picking up the loose change.

"Owning and running a bakery is a hard way to make a living—bad hours. Women were never bakers back then, so I never considered it. Mom, having been a nurse, encouraged me to go into medicine."

Debbie, the second daughter, also worked at the bakery but not as much as Tom and Jennifer did in their respective decades. She was there mostly during the holiday rush. Debbie was a child of the 1960s, which included loving to dress in long skirts, wearing beads and playing the guitar. She went to beautician's school.

Debbie, unfortunately, died in 1974 at the young age of twenty-one when she was hit by a car while riding a bike on Hanley Road. As anyone who has lost a child knows, her death broke Cindy's and Howard's hearts.

Luckily for all of us, Tom ended up following in his father's footsteps—after a slight detour. Continuing the Thie family recipe for success, Tom worked in the bakery throughout his childhood and high school years. Similar to the suggestions Cindy offered Jenny, Tom's mother encouraged him to consider going into the medical field, but Tom had no interest in becoming a doctor. Instead, after graduating from Colerain High School, Tom went to Ohio State for college and earned a degree in business. After his graduation in 1983, he returned to the bakery for two years until his interest in the preparation of food expanded, leading him to the prestigious Culinary Institute of America (CIA) in Hyde Park, New York, where he trained and graduated in 1987. Following this accomplishment, Tom was the sous chef at Commander's Palace in New Orleans (an old, traditional restaurant where Paul Prudhomme began his career), where he worked from 1987 to 1989 with the well-known Emeril Lagassé before Emeril started his own restaurant and became famous. Upon Tom's return to Cincinnati, he participated in the opening of the Phoenix Restaurant, along with fellow CIA graduate and chef Paul Sturkey. After a brief two months, Tom returned to the bakery to help his family when Cindy found out she had cancer.

In 1990, Tom married Cliftonite Maureen Sheppard, and they lived above the bakery until 1998, when they moved to White Oak. Moe, as she later became known, grew up in Clifton and had first come into the bakery as a little girl with her mother on their weekly Wednesday trips. She clearly remembers "the older baker, who turned out to be [her] father-in-law, bringing out a piece of bread or a Virginia reel" to give to her. In 1975, at the age of fourteen, Moe wanted to help her family after her father

Howard and son. Can you tell I liked this guy?

CIA graduation. A proud father and a happy son. I received seven honors that day.

died. With some assistance from a conversation between her mother and Marianne Wullenweber, one of the counter ladies, Moe was recommended and hired as one of the store girls in the front retail shop of the bakery. At that time, Tom was in college, but he worked on weekends as the delivery boy, and Moe helped him with the wedding cakes. She thought Tom, with his long blond hair, was very cute; he, in turn, liked her enough to tease her about being so short and gave her the nickname of "Midget."

Moe graduated from St. Ursula School, the University of Cincinnati, where she got an associate's degree in social work, and Cincinnati State, where she earned her degree as a dietetic technician. After earning her degree, Moe worked at Christ Hospital for twelve years. In 1993, Moe became more involved again with bakery work. She had grown very close to her mother-in-law, and when Cindy became ill, Moe was there to help. Cindy had built an outstanding wedding cake business, and she wanted to pass on that skill to her daughter-in-law. Moe began a demanding schedule, working at the hospital during the day and at the bakery during the night. In the course of a three-week period during which she was very sleep deprived, Moe iced one man's cake with the center icing thicker than the layers of cake. The customer came back in to say that while he liked sweets, this had been a little over the top.

On an evening when Cindy felt very ill and had to go to the hospital, Moe was left in the scary position of having to finish a wedding cake by herself. Moe was later terrified when she first started handling the wedding cake business on her own after Cindy died. "I didn't really know what I was doing. I didn't really know how to decorate, so how was I going to sell my first cake?" Whether she would have been comforted or more unsettled is unknown, but neighborhood customers had been thrilled when Moe joined the Virginia Bakery family and were later thrilled upon hearing the wedding cake operation had been passed along to a Clifton native. Despite the fact that there hadn't been much time for Cindy to teach all that she knew, Moe and Tom were able to make a success of the business. In 2002, Moe passed an examination held at Sinclair College in Dayton, earning her qualification as a Certified Master Cake Decorator from the National Retail Bakers' Association, and held double duty by working at Virginia Bakery and serving as an instructor at Bakery Hill, a division of the Midwest Culinary Institute at Cincinnati State College.

Under Tom's leadership, Virginia Bakery followed all the time-honored traditions: using fresh ingredients and quality products in its baked goods; being involved with the Bakers' Association (Tom was also on the GCRBA

To Be a Thie

Moe when she first started decorating cakes. *Courtesy of St. Ursula Academy of Walnut Hills, Cincinnati, Ohio.*

Board of Directors); and participating in community efforts, such as the Bread Fest, which provided bakery goods for less privileged people. The bakery was also involved with Toys for Tots and made weekly food donations to the Over-the-Rhine Soup Kitchen and the Clifton Senior Center. The Thies were also good about sharing whatever was needed with competitors and colleagues. If another baker, for example, ran out of flour in the middle of the night, he could call Tom and borrow some.

New under Tom's management was the introduction of computer technology, for which he received a leadership award in July 1995 from *Modern Baking*, one of the trade magazines, for recognition of the new business practices he initiated during his tenure. The steps he took improved the bookkeeping system for the bakery's continued growth and success. Tom created his own software programs that enabled his workers to type in price changes on a master price list that included approximately one hundred ingredients and three hundred finished products. He also put his made-from-scratch recipe formulas into the system so that he could easily adjust information as needed. Monthly, Tom compared invoices and price amounts, allowing him to pick out random items and check to be sure they were bringing in a profit. Being computerized also allowed him to produce his own advertisements as well as design his stationery and informational handouts, all of which saved a substantial amount of money. In addition, employee manuals and written job descriptions were created that let everyone know exactly what was expected of them, gave them responsibility and control and eliminated the possibility of excuses for work left undone.

Tom also took steps that increased time management by appointing people to manage the various departments of the back shops: the bread and rolls; coffee cakes; and cake and pastries departments. His typical personal work hours, for non-holiday months, were divided between the time frame from 4:00 a.m. to noon, when he worked in the production departments, and the rest of the day, which was spent in managing the business until roughly 3:00 p.m. By the mid-1990s, the bakery had twenty-three employees and gross sales reached $375,000.

As with previous generations, the relationship with Tom and Moe's employees was similar to an extended family. Kristine Kessler shared that they "definitely took me under their wing, and taught me how to decorate cakes and more!…Nothing could ever replace the time spent at the bakery and all of the growing up that I did while working there. They will always be my family." Annie Glenn is another person who became very close to the family as she, on occasion, took on the dual role as shop girl/babysitter when Carly would "assist" her with the jobs of cashiering and being a store clerk. And humor was always present and appreciated. "That's one thing I really miss," Tom says. "We worked hard, but I think we played harder. I can't tell you how many times I cried laughing."

The extended family atmosphere also was felt by their tenants. Tim Ruffner, who moved into one of the apartments above the bakery (living out one of this writer's fantasies) during his college years, described Moe and Tom as "wonderful, fantastic landlords…very open people, respectful, like a second set of parents." Tim most definitely felt he had moved into a warm place to live, both literally and figuratively. Both the delicious aromas and the oven heat found their way up the stairs, which was welcome in the winter and uncontrollable in the summer. The bond grew between them to the point that the Thies trusted him and his roommate, Kristin, to watch over things in the event of emergencies when they were out of town. With Moe's blessing, they were allowed to go downstairs into the bakery at night if they "ever wanted a little snack" and help themselves to items left in the closed cases. They went down a couple of times a week but also made a point of buying things on Saturdays. Moe also taught Tim some things about baking and decorating cakes, even letting him borrow some cake pans and have access to one of the apartment rooms that was filled with "boxes and boxes of cake decorating supplies." He remembers going in there to get a plastic baby when he made his first king cake.

"Carrying on an institution was a big responsibility," Moe shared, "but the neatest thing was how much people loved the place. While running the bakery with family was sometimes pretty difficult— personal and business things overlapping—and involved long, long hard hours, being known as the very best was very nice." Virginia Bakery provided "a wonderful experience, but working in the bakery becomes your whole life." Putting in eighty to ninety hours a week was not uncommon.

In the summer of 2000, the painful decision to close the full-service retail shop was made, and signs were mounted giving enough notice so that customers could come in and buy their favorite baked goods one last time. Tom admitted, in an interview with Chuck Martin for the *Cincinnati Enquirer*, that the decision was easier to make

Moe and Tom with a tray of schnecken, for which Virginia Bakery was famous. *Courtesy of the* Cincinnati Enquirer.

after his father had passed away. "'It breaks my heart to disappoint our loyal customers,' Mr. Thie said. But he said a severe shortage of skilled workers gave him little choice but to shut off the ovens." As Peter Houstle, executive vice-president of the Retailer's Bakery Association, explained, "Fewer and fewer people have baking skills…It takes a good three years to learn to bake. And fewer people are making that commitment." The labor problems created the concern that the quality of their products would go down and that customers would notice. Announcing the decision to the twenty employees was also very uncomfortable and distressing. While Tom felt confident that they would all be able to find employment, he did offer some assistance with the process of finding new work.

On August 8, after a well-deserved two-week vacation with their daughter Carly, Tom and Moe reopened Virginia Bakery as a wedding and specialty cake shop. Their decision was to concentrate on these cakes, which were more profitable. The change caused a period of adjustment for the two of them, going from being extremely busy and hectic to just the two of them in a much emptier and quieter space. Working between eight to ten hours a day became the shorter, less stressful schedule and allowed time to focus on making all sizes, shapes and styles of intricately decorated specialty cakes. By 2000, when they made this change, Moe had become quite accomplished at designing, baking and decorating custom cakes and had been making all the Virginia Bakery wedding cakes for almost ten years. Her business consisted mostly of private orders but also included contracts with the Omni Netherland Plaza hotel downtown and country clubs. On average, she made five wedding cakes a week but, on occasions, as many as seven. Each creation usually took between twelve and nineteen hours from start to finish, but there were times when Moe put in up to twenty-nine hours on a single cake. Her style and method was to be very particular with every detail.

Five years later, during the 2005 Labor Day weekend, a very unfortunate event happened and changed things dramatically. While Tom was trimming a large tree, a branch knocked the ladder from beneath him and he hit the ground hard. The fall resulted in a shattered vertebra and two severely fractured heels and ankles. The prognosis was not good: probable paralysis from the waist down, with severe loss of mobility and a possible amputation of the right foot. The decision to close Virginia Bakery was made that day. The sad resolution was made to rent the space that had been the family's bakery for so long. Again, to their credit, after Tom's accident, the decision was made to get word out to their customers so that they'd know there weren't going to be any schnecken available for the 2005 holiday season.

Fifth Generation of the Thie Bakery Family in the United States

Carly, Tom and Moe's daughter, can be attributed with saving her father's life. When he decided to climb a ladder and cut down a limb of an oak tree on their home property, she first told him he was too old to be doing such work but, if he was going to insist on doing the job, he should at least wear a bicycle helmet to protect his head. That advice paid off when the limb swung and knocked him to the street.

Carly's birth was anticipated by all of Virginia Bakery's regular customers months before she was born, and her arrival was celebrated when Moe proudly introduced her out front. As the daughter of parents who were working long hours in the bakery, Carly definitely grew up there. In the first months, seeing Moe working behind the counter with Carly in a baby sling

"Spin me again, Daddy."

or carrier was a natural sight. What customers did not get a glimpse of was Carly as an infant sleeping in the back in a huge bowl.

While Carly was a baby, Moe would put her in a back carrier. As they traveled around the bakery, Moe hadn't at first realized how Carly was going to swing around and reach out while on her back, just barely missing the variety of knobs, switches and very hot things that stuck out everywhere. The guys in the back shop started noticing this and would always joke that Moe was going to run her into one of those things. In response, one day Moe brought Carly into the back shop wearing a red colander with a purple ribbon securing it to her head—her first official crash helmet. Laughter ensued from all of the guys.

Carly shared a bowl story of her own. Tom had a "ginormous" metal bowl that was used for mixing sixty pounds of fruit at a time. When she was a toddler, he would put the bowl on the bench, pad the bottom of the bowl with aprons and put her in the bowl. Then, once she was all settled and safe, he would spin the bowl around and around, "like my own little carousel! I used to laugh and giggle." When the rotation would start to slow down, Tom would take her out of the bowl, and she would be so dizzy that her little legs would wobble all around. No negative side effects incurred. In fact, Carly was always a "happy kid."

Patty cake, patty cake, baker's man…

As Carly grew, she pitched in with the work at hand. While other children were going swimming, she was helping at the cash register and putting dots of icing on cakes when her mother was swamped. Never complaining, during the holidays she would help her grandmother, Moe's mother, for hours and hours.

On my mom's side of the bakery, she had her bench and there was a bench that was smaller and taller (we called it the egg table—it's typically where my dad would separate the egg whites from the egg yolks). Well, we would be on the side of the bench opposite my mom. When I was really young (about four years old), all I could do was fold up the boxes, but then as I started getting older I learned to cut and wrap gems, as well as how to fold the wax paper to wrap schnecken and how to tie up boxes with the famous red and white string. I was taught to tie schnecken boxes before I was taught how to tie shoes!

Fun things happened at the bakery, too. Having Aunt Jenny come to visit "her" Carly was always a treat, and the spot where Tom wrote Carly's name in a wet cement square of sidewalk by the back door is evidence of times that weren't all work.

Carly, at five years old, was also quite mature for her age and, as it turned out, ready to help in an emergency. One time when Moe was going in to finish up some wedding cakes for the weekend, she started to close the parking lot gate, became distracted and turned to look at something. The gate started rolling, and Moe's hand got caught—resulting in a portion of her finger being badly cut and hanging. Nicole, one of the employees, drove them to the hospital. While in the examining room, Nicole got a glimpse of Moe's hand and fainted. Little Carly immediately went to the door and shouted, "We need a nurse, we need a nurse!"

While what the future holds, especially for Carly, is yet to be known, surely her life will be filled with the rewards of her experiences, which are in part the result of being a member of the Thie family.

Shop Stories

Back in the day, the Thies' old-fashioned German bakery was just one of hundreds of family bakeries in the Greater Cincinnati area, and yet theirs always stood out as having an excellent and unique reputation. While many people thought of Virginia Bakery as a high-end bakery, the bakery was not a fancy place. Instead, as Bill Pritz (a former employee and now owner of his own Shadeau Breads) explained, Virginia Bakery was "more of an everyday place where there was an emphasis on quality. It had a lot of value on an ordinary level, and I was attracted to and inspired by that." Virginia Bakery was a full line bakery that made approximately three hundred items, including various breads, cookies, cakes and pastries, from scratch. This traditional bakery made things according to recipes, not mixes, and they did not add "a lot of strange things" (artificial ingredients). Mr. Pritz added, "The profession has changed. While back then it was just a bakery using an expected common method, anything like it now is considered an artisan bakery because they don't use mixes. New bakeries have caved in—given up on their standards—not a good choice."

As is true of all enterprises, over the years Virginia Bakery had to continually adjust to the ever-shifting social climate. Some of the changes were effortless; others were exceedingly challenging. Regardless, all of the adaptations were essential for survival, from the first generation to the last. Tom's grandfather's concerns dealt with the cost of raw materials and having to constantly haggle with vendors. His parents actually enjoyed the heyday, being able to get raw materials and labor fairly easily without having to provide insurance. With Tom, attracting and retaining laborers was the problem. Most people did not want to work the awful hours, and many wanted to be hired for a wage well above minimum while not having much schooling in the trade. As Tom told Bob Driehaus during a July 2000 interview for the *Cincinnati Post*, "All over the country, there is a complete lack of bakers in training right now, and small bakeries are closing left and right." In addition, a lack of medical or retirement packages made working there unattractive. A small family operation could not compete with the big places that were able to afford providing pensions. So it was for Virginia Bakery.

Before the doors were permanently closed, Virginia Bakery was a wonderland of delicious baked goods for the loyal and devoted customers who appreciated the Thies' traditional, complete operation of making everything from scratch with the finest ingredients. The many hours of hard work that took place in the family-like atmosphere of the back rooms were definitely worthwhile. The Virginia Bakery legacy lives on in memories.

Retail Shop

If you happened into the bakery during the 1950s, you would have seen a green/black art deco–influenced exterior. The newer appearance of the red-painted brick exterior with white trim and the Virginia Bakery logo on the side of the building overlooking the parking lot took place in the 1980s. In the early 1950s, the interior was also given a fresh look. Up until the renovation, there had been two exterior display windows, one on each side of the storefront. Following the changes, the large window on the right side was opened up for viewing into the store, and the angular window by the door on the left became the single outdoor display area. The seasonal and themed window displays, whether created under Myrtle, Cindy or Moe's charge, were always eye-catching and clever and frequently discussed among customers waiting to be called up to the counter.

Once you opened the door and entered the shop, the enticing aroma of freshly baked breads, cakes and cookies filled the air, and you were likely to smile when you breathed in the combined sweet smells of sugary yeast dough, butter, cinnamon and vanilla, among others. The very first thing to do was take a ticket from the dispenser by the door. To children accompanying their parents, being chosen to press down the handle and remove the ticket was a big deal, often requiring a lift or a prearranged scheduled order among

Art deco exterior of the bakery's early years.

This is the Virginia Bakery's exterior after its 1980s remodel. *Courtesy of Tim Ruffner.*

The Thie ladies took pride in their window displays.

siblings for the weekly visits. Getting your number was a definite necessity. The bakery was always crowded; customers filled the store. Dick Nichols, part owner of C&L Motors, which used to be next to Virginia Bakery, was quoted in the July 2009 *Valley Courier* newspaper as saying that he remembers Virginia Bakery was "a very neat and clean operation…On Saturday mornings, it was impossible to park near the bakery. Many times we would let people park on the lot waiting to hear their number called. Virginia Bakery had a great business and people came from all parts of the city to buy bread, rolls and coffee cakes. Many times I sold a car to people who were waiting to have their number called."

While you waited in anticipation with your number in hand, you gazed at all the glass display counter cases and side cabinets filled and brimming with rows of tempting pastries and breads of various shapes and colors, which hinted at the various flavors and textures promised within each bite. Other things could catch your eye, too. There were the figurines for topping birthday cakes, as well as some wedding cake decorations, displayed on a high top shelf along the back wall under the art deco trim. And below that was the well-known big round blue tinted mirror, which is currently hanging in Carly Thie's bedroom. While some (now grownup) children wondered if the staff members were watching them in the reflection, the counter

Carly can't believe how dressed up the ladies were in 1942 just to go shopping. If someone can explain that to her, please e-mail us.

ladies remember getting a kick out of watching people come in and check themselves out in the blue mirror.

When your number was called, you ordered the favorite cake or Danish that you had been "mentally guarding" as quickly as possible, saving the things you saw multiple choices of for after you captured the prized item. Going there and seeing someone else buy the last one of something right in front of you or finding that they were out of something you'd been craving, actually already salivating over, was extremely disappointing. On those occasions, you might have tried a new item that you'd just overheard other people raving about. For the most part, though, consistent customers had their family favorites. Members of the Mohan family were impressed by the fact that the counter ladies who had been there and known customers "forever" knew exactly what the regulars were going to pick out on their weekly visits, even the favorite pastry of each family member.

Virginia Bakery's friendly atmosphere was, according to Bill, another of his secrets for success. He knew that in addition to men in the back who were skilled and knowledgeable in their trade and using quality products to make a large variety of items throughout the day, storefront employees who were friendly and efficient when helping customers was also an important component. Being a weekly stop, the bakery and the counter ladies became very familiar, and everyone, young and old, found the shop to be a happy, comfortable place where you were likely to run into at least one person you knew. The clerks were familiar—mostly mature matronly types, along with a few high school and college students. The retail shop workers, some having worked there for twenty, thirty, even forty years—such as Esther Billman, Virginia Hasslinger Gardner, Emily Kaderli, Stella Kaiser, Gert Moore, Theresa Nacke, Cora Samad, Charlotte Siegler and Marian Wullenweber—were originally required to wear uniforms with fancy handkerchiefs stuck in the front pockets and little hats or head pieces. As time went on and more casual clothes were generally accepted, many of the shop girls switched to wearing official Virginia Bakery white T-shirts with the bakery's red logo.

Novices to the retail shop duties usually started by filling cases and keeping them clean, filling orders and waiting on customers. For those who stayed and had the desire and talent, there were additional responsibilities and promotions available. As Kristine Kessler shared, "I started out as a store girl, waiting on customers, running the cash register, repacking shelves, wrapping schnecken, slicing bread…and the list goes on. But as the years went on, I…became the cookie decorator and soon after the cake decorator." Helen Adams expressed benefits gained from working at Virginia Bakery. "That job taught me many invaluable lessons. I learned the obvious things about responsibility, the value of a dollar and respect for your superiors. It also taught me what it is like to be in retail during the holiday season. To this day I try to show kindness and express gratitude to the people I encounter who are in the trenches during the stressful holiday season. I have great empathy for them."

Most of the ladies who worked out front stayed a long time—most likely because they enjoyed working for the Thies and with one another, and perhaps the bonus of being able to easily access the baked goods. Because there was not much of a turnover, their faces were often familiar to customers from childhood through adulthood. Relationships were built, and these ladies knew all of the regular customers by their first names. Some customers came into the store only wanting certain people, their friends, to wait on them. When patterns were developed, hearing something like, "Bob, I've got just the thing for you—the bran muffins just came out of the oven, but there's some good bread and coffee cakes left over from weekend" was not uncommon. In a few rare cases, outgoing customers like Mel Rueger and his buddies felt so at home that they would step behind the counters and, while joking around, start "helping" to sell things. For fifteen minutes or so, they became part of the crowd working there. Sometimes salesmen who had

Front counter ladies sing that song. Do Da! This is at a party? Could they be any happier?

been servicing the store for long periods of time would also go out to the storefront and visit behind the counter. Friendships even developed to the point that customers, like Bob Schawann and his wife, would stop in to see an employee when she was at home sick.

Although sharing stories between workers and customers happened throughout the year, during the holidays in particular, customers enjoyed relating their bakery memories with the clerks. Cora Samad's grandchildren shared the memory of going to her home on Sundays and listening to her as she proudly showed them her beautiful white aprons and happily told stories about her work at the bakery. As the result of hearing about the events, "sometimes we felt like we knew everyone there also."

While the Virginia Bakery staff was for the most part very welcoming and efficient, there were a few of the ladies who seemed gruff and not so friendly at times. Jenny Thie remembers a person who had that opinion and once made the comment that the older ladies at the bakery should have hooked up with the old German waiters at Mecklenburg's restaurant, who were known for being pretty ornery and cantankerous. That might not have been a bad idea. Another customer remembered seeing one of the grumpy old ladies turn charming when an older gentleman became her next customer.

Once your number was called, the counter lady asked what you would like. This was also the moment she would offer a free cookie to any young child accompanying an adult. If you had come in with the hopes of buying a particular item that was not on display, checking in "the back" to find out what times various baked goods would be finished baking was part of the routine. Depending on the answer, a quick trip to a neighboring store might have filled the gap in time, or else another trip in a couple hours would take place.

As items were selected, the salespeople would pick up the cakes, rolls or pastries with waxed paper and place them in the appropriate box. There were different boxes for specific uses: for example, coffee cakes and a large order of sweet rolls fit in the square boxes; tea cookies and schnecken were put in the deeper rectangular ones. There was an art to tying the string, too. Annie Glenn explained, "Learning to 'gift wrap' the official white Virginia Bakery box with red-and-white string was introduced early as an employee. In a given day of work, I would tie a lot of boxes! I got so quick at each 'wrap' that I remember, instead of cutting the string with scissors, I broke the string with a quick tug/rip. Tying a box fast was essential to working there. Especially on a busy Saturday morning."

As each box was filled, the saleslady would write down the cost on a small piece of paper. When everything you wanted for the day had been chosen, the slip of paper was tucked under the string on your top box and you headed over to the cash register. Barbara Weishaar remembers, before newer equipment was bought, using the old cash register that "was just a regular cash register. You had to add up the total in your head."

In Virginia Bakery's early years, standing orders or calling in orders didn't exist, unless one counts a mother or grandmother saying something like, "While you're out, stop at Virginia Bakery and get…" Later, the in-store order department was established for those people who didn't need to look into the glass cases to choose their items because they knew what they wanted days ahead of purchase. This process, for the most part, guaranteed that you got the particular items you wanted, but it did not always guarantee that the trip would be all that much faster. Due to the crowds, picking up placed orders could also take time. Christmas was extreme, but the order department was always busy. "We never sat down on Saturdays, never," remembers Karen Striet. "If we got lunch, it would be because somebody ran over to Skyline, and we'd eat it standing up. The amount of orders they took in was incredible. There would always be about ten people waiting in line."

The new "Thesco" cases are shown off in this 1940s interior shot.

The wall cases are still in the building.

A view of the 1950s interior of the store. *Photographed by Gini Saas.*

Orders taken by phone would begin to be filled early on Saturday mornings, as soon as the store clerks arrived. There were little index cards with the orders written on them, and the ladies started filling them as quickly as things came out of the ovens. That procedure led to an incredible quantity of boxed items stacked on racks. Similarly handled, standing orders were ones where people got the same baked goods every week—for example, they'd always want a large loaf of whole wheat bread sliced and an apple coffee cake. Once in a while, the customers might have changed the coffee cake after they came in, but they usually kept things the same. The alphabetically ordered cards, which were kept in a special spot by the racks, would get worn out over time. When handling coffee cakes and then touching the cards, the ladies were likely to get a little bit of sticky fruit or butter goo on them. Once in a while, some cards would get misplaced, and at those times, customers were upset: "What do you mean you don't have it; I ordered it!"

Bake Shops

While the retail shop had the delectable aroma and display of finished products, the bake shops had their own visual and aromatic settings of baked goods in production. Because of the store's floor plan, you had the ability to view the bakers and cake decorators at work in the center areas, known as the "front shop" to the employees. Looking farther back, you saw another workspace, the "back shop," which was on a level about three feet higher than the rest of the bakery and reached via a ramp. An article titled "Schneckens Take to the Mail" in the Cincinnati Bakery Tour section of the February 1989 trade journal *Bakery* noted, "The shop's arrangement allows the departments to work separately and enables the bakers to make their wide assortment on a near-daily basis. The back room is devoted to yeast-product processing, and a reel oven maintains the temperatures needed for breads that come out at 1 p.m. A separate oven in the pastry department [front shop] allows Howard and an assistant to bake cakes and pastries needed to fill orders." When standing in the retail shop, to the left was the room where phone orders were stacked and cakes were decorated. On the right side, lots of lively activity was visible through the doorway and through the open spaces of the tall racks that held loaves and loaves of bread and huge racks of other baked goods that had been brought down from the back shop ready for sale. Sweaty bakers, covered with flour (as was everything else) and talking very loudly over the noise of some of the equipment, were busy at work kneading dough, stirring huge pots and handling heavy trays hot from the ovens. Barbara Weishaar remembers the bakers making all of the items every day in that space. "Things were fresh, continually brought out from the back."

In the very beginning of the Thies' Clifton bakery, there was just a small kitchen with only an oven, a mixer and a baker, Bill. By 1950, when Hattie was interviewed by Clementine Paddleford, the shops had grown and there were six bakers besides the family members. Over weekends, the baking started at 4:00 a.m. on Fridays and kept going until 6:00 p.m. on Saturday evenings. In 1999, Polk Laffoon described the operation in his article for the *Cincinnati Post*:

> For people who have never seen the Virginia Bakery, it is best to imagine either a very large Mom and Pop business or a very small factory. [Bill] Thie employs "somewheres over" 20 people, all working like a Red Cross relief crew, and Thie is in the thick of it…He laughs about the hook he

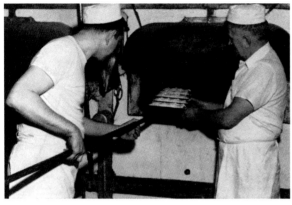 

Bill is holding a customer favorite, the single-layer cake. He truly was a master. He loved his work. *Courtesy of the General Mills Archives.*

uses to retrieve rolls from the back of the oven, explaining that it came from the Empress or Olympic Burlesque (he can't remember which)—it was the hook they used to pull lousy acts offstage. "When the women wore tights, all the bakers went down to see them," he confided.

The environment of the back shops was warm—both literally and figuratively. Bill Pritz described the shops as providing an engaging environment. "The walls were plaster—a real solid old building that had a reassuring, comfortable way about it—a bit of a holdout from a previous era." The rooms were filled with shelving and racks, a jumble of bowls (some 80 quarts big), giant whisks, huge powerful mixers (110-quart size) that stood on the floor and commanded respect, sinks, wood tables and metal pans. The smooth-topped, long wooden preparation tables from the 1920s had seen years of dough banging, kneading and rolling. Every spot had a purpose in the tight quarters. There were areas for scaling off the ingredients, mixing, sheeting, adding fillings, proofing, baking, frying and giant ovens (the big, older one in the back was similar to a pizza oven; the one in the front shop had four rotating shelves), which were so hot that the heat could be felt feet away from the closed oven doors. By comparison, the area where the orders were kept and the finishing work of icings and frostings was done was pleasantly cool.

The Thie family and their employees had a special relationship with their work. The cast of characters (approximately twenty at any given

WEEK-END RUSH. Baking starts at four a.m. on Friday

Photographed by Norman Gordon. Courtesy of Black Star.

time) employed there formed an efficient team made up of members who knew and carried out their particular responsibilities and seemed to really enjoy the work, while at the same time creating a family atmosphere among themselves. "There was an integrity to it—a focus on craft—something a person had to learn over a period of years to become good at," Bill Pritz explained. Jerry Armstead proudly corroborates that idea.

> *That's a trade. Nowadays, everything is made on a conveyor belt—all the parts are brought in, like the icing is brought in. Tom's dad made icing every day, all fresh. Everything that came out of those mixing bowls went on that table, and we did it by hand…everything. We rolled the bread, rolled the schnecken—you name it. After that we put items in the proof box that activated the yeast and then popped them in the oven. Working at Virginia Bakery made you versatile. We did it all. Everything now is automated and made in a rush. We took our time with the process.*

Similarly time was, and remained, a factor in the progression of jobs that led to becoming a baker. Oftentimes, young men started out being hired to clean the back shops or as dishwashers and then moved on to bench work and progressed to learning the oven as they worked their way up to become a baker. Watching the oven entailed taking prepared products, putting them in the oven, taking them out of the oven and then giving them to the person who would ice them. Eventually, with more experience, workers learned how to measure and mix the ingredients. Most bakers were, and still are, very secretive about their recipes. Workers might have been shown steps one through four and then sent out for some eggs and, when they returned, found steps five through seven already completed. Then, as now, the steps involved were isolated. A "mixer" did his work, someone who did "makeup work" did his and the two did not see how the other job was being accomplished, so neither of them knew the whole recipe or steps involved.

The front shop was where all the cakes, pies and icings were made. Ed Arnult and his brother J.D. started their employment at Virginia bakery when Bill Thie was "The Boss" and Carl was in charge of the front shop. Ed remembers that working there was hard work but felt that doing so was good training, and he appreciated the experience. "There was a lot to do and most of it had to be done fast in order to get it done." He helped with cake pans. After they were washed by the porter, he would usually grease them so that they'd be ready for the next day. He also helped in the preparation of cake mixes—getting the sugar and flour and other ingredients together and bringing up additional ingredients from storage in the basement. The basement was where the apples were peeled and the eggs were cracked. "Sometimes I'd get to help dish out cake stuff, but usually Carl did that. He'd weigh them. Most ingredients were measured by weight and visually. You'd get pretty good after a while knowing what, for example, five pounds of lard looked like." Ed also "learned how to tell when the cakes were ready to come out of the oven by the look and touch of things. Early on, I'd have Carl check my decisions about taking things out." Gus Nolte, also an employee when Bill was in charge, worked in both shops. He came in very early and did some stuff in the back but primarily worked with Carl up front.

When Howard came back from the navy, he worked the front shop, taking over Carl's responsibilities. Cakes, pies, sometimes cookies during the holidays and all the icings were made on this lower level. They, along with the cake decorating (which had previously been done by a cousin, Marion Maujer), were his concentration. Back by the oven was where all the cakes Howard made sat to cool.

This is how you know when things are done. Bill is lightly pressing on the cake. If it springs back, you've got it. *Photographed by Norman Gordon. Courtesy of Black Star.*

The back shop was where everything else was made. While Carl ran the front shop, Bill was overall in charge in the back and working full time with his son, Paul, making breads, doughnuts, coffee cakes, schnecken, butter bits and a variety of pastries.

During that era, there was a cousin, also named Bill Thie, who worked mostly in the back shop. To differentiate between the two, he was known as

The young master at work. Howard could decorate as well as bake.

"old Price Hill Bill." Ed saw him pull things out of the oven with his bare hands. The response to "You can't do that!" was "Yeah you can, after you get used to it. You have to grab them fast." Charlie Hensey was also an oven man. His main job was to load up the oven and take things out at the right time— just as with the items baked in the front shop, by the look and touch of them. Charlie used a big flat paddle type board, similar to what you might see in a pizza place, to pull baked goods out. Then he'd "dump" the items out onto the metal dump rack before being put on the shelving racks.

Ed recalled the square pans used for coffee cakes and how he would dump those out and put the cakes on a shelving rack. When full, two people (one in front and one in back—"Bill used to like to be in the front") would carry the racks down "the chicken run" (a narrow little ramp between the two levels that had boards going across every so often to keep the men with wet shoes from slipping on flour) to the front. As they rushed down past the steps to the basement, they'd be yelling "Hot stuff! Coming through!" so people on the lower level would get out of the way. "If anybody was in front of the oven, they'd have to move. Whoever was leading the rack would slide it into the storing shelving. They'd come flying down—I don't know why they always had to do it so fast, but they did." Perhaps for show? Lou Dorsey, a baker at Virginia Bakery for over fifty years, described the activity in the back shop as hectic to his family.

After the cakes had been dumped, there would be residue on the edges of the pans, so the next job was to take a scraper and remove the sticky remainders. The pans were not washed, however, because they needed to remain seasoned. Instead, they were stacked up high, and all this was done at a very quick speed. Ed added, "After a while, you wouldn't even have to look; you'd just flip them up after they were scraped. Without looking they'd just go where they were supposed to go and fall into place where they should. You had to do things fast in the bakery."

George Ashford was the porter in the back for a very long time. After he died, his son worked there for a while. George's job was to clean anything that did need to be washed in a big sink. Using a metal scraper to pick up all the ingredients that had fallen off the tables and cooling racks, he also cleaned the floor. Another porter, Jim Turner, worked with Carl, Howard and then Tom in the front shop taking care of the cake and pie pans.

All the bakers were men, and quite a few of them were from Germany. Fritz Pieper was one of the ones who had grown up in Germany. Despite their strong accents, for the most part they spoke English pretty well. Ron stated, "You could understand them, but some interesting language situations did occur." On one occasion, one of the German bakers tripped over an empty egg crate that had been left on the ramp. As he fell over, he grabbed the banister and saved himself from falling down the basement steps. Although safe from harm, he was very upset that someone had left the crate in the wrong place, which, in turn, had caused him to fall. As a result, he said angrily, "That was due to someone's negligee!"

Other interesting language situations came about because there was an employee who was deaf and mute; he could not hear or speak. He was affectionately known as "Dumby." He only spoke in sign language, so several of the other workers learned how to spell words, letter by letter, with their right hands. "Red"—not Howard, who had that nickname in high school, but Louis Suhre, who iced cakes—was also hearing impaired. Red wore a hearing aid, but it didn't do much for him. As a result, he became great at reading lips. He could see people across the street at the gas station and if they were talking he could pretty accurately tell the other bakers what they said.

Customers remember seeing the guys laughing and having fun in the back. They were hard at work, but there seemed to be a lot of camaraderie. Jerry said:

Yeah, we had a lot of fun all day long. We used to play jokes on each other. There was one guy who came in later—most of them came in real early, but he'd come in around 6:00 a.m. When he'd come in, we'd all be standing there as he went downstairs to change his clothes. There were two stairways to the basement. One day, I went down the other way, put on a mask and came up behind him and scared him. I wanted to get him because that man used to eat some of my food.

Ed remembered a prank pulled on some of the counter ladies on occasion. The ladies' restroom was in the back shop. Every now and then, George would come by with a big stack of metal pans while a lady was in the bathroom and he'd drop them on the floor right by the door. "You should have seen them come out of there!"

The back shops of the bakery were hot, and that was one of the reasons Ron was not a huge fan of working at the bakery. Standing between a wall and a big oven, with towels wrapped around his forehead and his neck to keep from sweating on the coffee cakes while he put icing on them, was not fun for him. The back shops of a bakery can't have air conditioning because of the impact on dough. To be staring at a thermometer that read 120 or 125 degrees in the summer was not uncommon. The winter was slightly better. Ron Thie chuckled, though, as he shared how he was taught, as probably all bakers have been, to use his hands when he iced these items. "You can do a whole tray worth of tea rings in the time it would take to ice half a cake with a spatula." While it is the most efficient and quickest method, his wife and her friends get upset when he currently tries to help them ice bazaar cakes.

By the smile, you wouldn't know how hard he worked.

With the bakery being such a hot spot, bakers could often be seen standing at the back screened door getting some fresh, cooler air. Another popular answer for a lot of the bakers was to drink beer in the back. (Maybe it's that baker's yeast connection!) "The guys liked to drink their beer—not to the point of being too much—they just enjoyed it in moderation," Ed stated. Back in the early 1940s when he worked there as a teenager, his first job every day was to go on a beer run. He would get a big broomstick, with the broom part cut off, and then he'd go into the back shop. Each man would give him his beer bucket and give Ed his order. One might say he wanted twenty cents' worth and the next might say twenty-five cents' worth, and so forth. Ed would end up with about (no more than) four aluminum buckets on the stick and go over to the College Inn (between the Firehouse and Pete's News Stand) and tell the bartender how much was supposed to go into each bucket. He was able to buy the beer even though he was in high school. Nobody questioned it. Obviously, he wasn't supposed to buy any for himself, but they all said he could drink out of any of their buckets. He didn't do it much. "I didn't feel right about it…Gus enjoyed his beer. Being in the front shop, a lot of the customers standing out in the store could see him, so he enjoyed doing a little singing and putting on a little show—just about the time he'd had enough beer!" Lou Dorsey and Lou Fal seemed to be the exceptions at that time. They just drank Pepsi.

The beer tradition carried on for years. Ron also remembered seeing somebody sent out to a bar in Corryville around 10:00 a.m. and coming back with half-gallon jugs of tapped beer. This hour was about the time some of them started to eat lunch. The beer would be all gone by the time they left around 1:00 to 3:00 p.m. "I never saw anybody get drunk; they probably sweated out most of it." Tom remembered other stories about someone taking empty five-gallon milk cans up to Fries Café on Jefferson Avenue, having them filled up and bringing them back. One day, one of the guys (who perhaps had already drunk too much) didn't clean out the can well (leaving spoiled milk in it) and had them fill it up. All the men got sick.

A happier five-gallon can story dealt with Charlie, the oven man, who used to make an eggnog during the holidays in which he would add a fifth of whiskey and a fifth of something else. No doubt the beverage was a welcome gift after many, many hours of intense work. Jerry stated,

There were good times and bad times, but during the holiday time of year, they used to work us to death. During holiday seasons, the schedule was very difficult. Howard would say, "I hope you guys aren't making any plans."

From October to January, it was constant—orders for schnecken, cookies, butter bits—everything people wanted on their tables during the celebration season. Every day was nonstop. Even on the days the bakery was closed, we came in to make cookies and schnecken. We had to give people what they wanted.

Except for the gifts of a ham or a turkey to all the employees, the tales above could be loosely interpreted as "Don't even think you're going to celebrate." A story shared by Ellen Sibert underscores the intensity of the holiday workload. "My father, Berthold Schwegmann, had to work the day I was born, as it was six days before Christmas…When he got the call from the hospital that I had been born, they allowed him to jump up and down on a table and hoot and holler. [Throughout my life] I was always told that I was born at a terrible time for the bakery business."

Tom summed up the situation when he said in the bakery business there is a brotherhood, coupled with awful hours and hard work. "Being a baker, you love it and you hate it. Work sometimes started about 1:00 a.m. and we worked until the job was done. The typical day of a baker was eight to twelve hours when including doing the books after baking work finished. Your workers are usually willing to put in the hard work if they see you do the same." And Tom certainly set an example: he worked on the days both of his parents died.

Before You Bake

Please take a moment to read over the following information.

Brown Sugar

For any recipe calling for brown sugar, use light brown sugar.

Butter

Except for the schnecken recipe, all of the Virginia Bakery recipes use salted butter.

I know a lot of people may be alarmed about the amount of butter we used, but that's what makes our stuff so good. Through all the fat research of the last couple decades, butter has fared well, when consumed in moderation, compared to its counterparts.

Butter Wash

When a recipe says to wash with butter, use a mixture of half melted butter and half vegetable oil to wash doughs.

Corn Syrup

For any recipe calling for corn syrup, use light corn syrup.

The corn syrup is used to either provide a nice shine, as in a glaze; to help bind, as in some of the fillings; or to extend shelf life.

Doneness

The number one question, "How do you know when it's done?" has only one correct answer. The answer is "When it's done." The variables are too many to give exact times. Your dough temperature, the air temperature and your oven temperature are but a few. You have to remember that baking is an old art, one that existed before techno gadgets. Early bakers relied on their senses and made some incredible stuff, which is what we are trying to keep alive here. The times and temperatures given in this book are mere guidelines.

Home ovens vary greatly, and oven thermometers are not that accurate. They can vary by ten degrees either way. You need to use your eyes and sense of touch to check for doneness. A clock can't do this; it can only get you in the ballpark.

Most doughs have one thing in common: you can feel if they are done baking. If you press on dough while it is still baking, you can tell if it's done. If you press on the dough and it doesn't spring back, it's not done. It's that simple. By combining your sense of sight and sense of touch you will always know how long to bake something.

Don't open and close the oven. Every time you open that door you lose at least twenty-five degrees of oven heat. When you close the oven door, your oven compensates by turning on the heat, which commonly comes from the bottom. What happens is you begin to technically sauté the dough, cooking more on one side, as in a skillet. By the time your item appears done on top, it will probably be burnt on the bottom. A better method, if you have checked and the items are not done, is to shut off the oven, leave them in and let the residual heat cook them a few minutes more.

Eggs

Unless otherwise stated, when a recipe calls for an egg, use a large egg.

One egg yolk is approximately equal to 1 Tbs. So, ⅛ cup = 2 yolks; ¼ cup = 4 yolks; and so on.

Egg Wash

For egg wash, whisk one whole egg, add an equal amount of water and whisk again.

Flour

Flour is spooned into the measuring cups and is not sifted. Once in the cup, level off the flour with the flat edge of a knife.

Measuring Sticky Stuff

A quick note about measuring sticky stuff like corn syrup, honey or molasses: if you are using another liquid, like milk, water, oil or eggs, measure the liquid first; then measure in the sticky stuff. The liquid will help keep it from sticking to the cup.

Also remember that 1 oz. = 2 Tbs. It is a lot easier to measure 1 oz. of corn syrup in a cup with another liquid than trying to measure 2 Tbs. of corn syrup with measuring spoons. One last thought: if you do like using the spoons, spray them with oil and the stuff won't stick as much either.

Milk

Virginia Bakery always used fresh whole milk, which I prefer. We're not making diet bakery goods. When you consider the amount of fat and eggs in the dough, changing the milk is not going to save many fat calories. On the other hand, if skim is all you have, use it. You can always compensate by adding a tad more butter.

Pan Dressing

When you put something in the pan before the dough, like schnecken goo or a butter mix, it is called "pan dressing."

Pan Sizes

A one-pound, three-ounce piece of bread dough fits in an 8" x 4" loaf pan; a one-pound, eleven-ounce piece fits a 9" x 5" loaf pan.

Proofing

Dough should not be exposed to open air while proofing, as it will develop a skin, which can cause ugly blotches on your finished product. In fact, dough should always be covered and not exposed to open air. This includes almost every step from mixing to storing. Air is a baked good's worst enemy.

Coffee cakes are the one exception to the rule; they do not need to be covered while proofing. The buttercream, cinnamon crumbs or fruit act as "the cover" for the dough; hence, it is not exposed to air.

Recipes

All the recipes in this book are provided and written by me, Tom Thie. We suggest that you read through the recipes to familiarize yourself with the needed ingredients and procedure before you start. Timing can be critical in baking.

Recipes are only guidelines that somebody wrote down. How accurate they are depends on who did the writing, as well as other factors. If you are using a recipe and it's not working, you may need to adjust it using some common sense. For example, a roll icing. There have been times when I have had to constantly adjust this recipe by either adding more powdered sugar or water to get the right consistency. If the icing was too thin, I would add more sugar. Too thick, more water. All recipes are like that. If the bread dough looked too thin, I'd add more flour. If the white roll dough looked too stiff, I'd add more milk.

Recipes have been changed and adjusted over time to get the desired final product. They are a set of instructions written by other people that happened to work for them in a particular setting at a particular time. It doesn't mean a given recipe will work for you, in your kitchen, your oven, on any particular day. Baking and cooking are about constantly tasting, observing and adjusting until you have the desired result.

Temperatures

When referring to liquids, cool is 70 degrees, warm is 105 degrees, hot is 110 degrees. Yeast will bloom or grow best around 105 degrees or in a warm liquid. If you put something on your lip and you can't feel it, it is around 98.6 degrees. In culinary circles, this temperature is known as "blood heat." If the liquid is warm, it's around 105. If it is hot or burns, it's over 110.

Historically, descriptive rather than numerical terms were used to indicate oven temperature: very slow 250 F, slow 300 F, moderately slow 325 F, moderate 350 F, moderately hot 375 F, hot 400 F and very hot 450–500F. Virginia Bakery's convention along these lines was to designate 350 F as low, 375 F as warm and 425 F as hot.

Using Your Senses

Baking is a sensual art, utilizing taste, smell, touch, sight and even hearing. Taste is probably the most important sense to a baker. Professionally, you need to constantly taste the product whether you want to or not.

Touch is also important in baking. Learn to use your hands. This is a hands-on art, which is why I like it so much. God gave you a thermometer, cake tester, dough divider, bread kneader and pair of tongs all on one hand. Use them. Your hand can mix, portion, mold, sculpt, measure temperature and volume and feel for doneness far better than any high-priced gadget.

Utensils

Those of you who are new to baking from scratch might want to expand your collection of baking tools as you get more involved with the process.

- A bench scraper is a good tool to have on hand while making bread products.
- Although touch is the best and most accurate way to know if something is done, an instant thermometer can be useful for determining 190 to 200 internal degrees for bread and rolls.
- A pizza wheel cutter is handy for cutting strips of dough.
- A pastry bag is very useful for icings, as well as applying fillings in certain recipes.
- A frying thermometer is extremely helpful when making doughnuts.
- A handheld doughnut hopper can make forming some types of doughnuts much easier.
- A scale for measuring weight assures consistent results.
- A soft-haired brush removes excess flour gently.
- A mesh strainer for dusting confectioner's sugar produces an even, professional appearance.
- An offset spatula for icing cake makes the job easier.
- A peel, a flat baking or pizza board, is handy for removing syrup and custard pies from the oven, as well as for when baking French bread on bricks.

Schnecken

"Will the schnecken recipe be included?" was the resounding refrain from people when they heard *Virginia Bakery Remembered* was being written.

"A heavenly morsel," "a golden brick of pastry" and "outstanding confection" were just some of the phrases used to describe Virginia Bakery's schnecken, its "crown" item. Without a doubt, schnecken ranked as the most well known, most popular and celebrated baked good by the time the bakery closed. As such, this chapter is dedicated to schnecken alone.

The name "schnecken" was derived from the German word for snail and was no doubt chosen because of how the dough is curled into rolls before being snugly fit into pans. Tom jokes that schnecken are nothing more than sugar and butter, with just enough flour to hold the mixture all together. Obviously, there's a little more to the process for Virginia Bakery to have reached such a level of success and to be known as, as Chuck Martin wrote in 1999 for the *Enquirer*, "the most famous Schnecken factory in town, if not the country."

Tom is not sure whether the recipe came over from Germany with his great-grandfather or was created on American soil; regardless, Virginia Bakery has made schnecken the old-fashioned way since at least 1927, meaning by hand, because this is a product that can't be properly made with mixers. The bakers blended cinnamon, sugar and raisins and spread them over a buttered sheet of rich, sweet dough. The dough was then rolled and cut. Three pieces of the roll were placed in a butter-lined pan and baked upside down until golden brown. When the schnecken were turned out from their molds (the bakery's term for schnecken pans), the sugar and butter had formed a rich caramel-like glaze, yielding an incomparable confection, especially when eaten warm from the oven.

As numerous aficionados reported, the true test of good schnecken, by Virginia Bakery standards, was that they had to be gooey to the degree that having the buttery glaze drip down one's chin when taking a bite was highly anticipated. Oftentimes, people chose to peel the layers or even eat the cake part separately, saving the topping to savor at the end.

Though introduced to Virginia Bakery customers many, many years earlier, schnecken's popularity exploded during the late 1950s and then again in the 1980s. All of a sudden the bakers couldn't make enough of them, a trend that continued until the store closed. Once people became introduced to them, they became hooked, often buying one weekly; these consumers never forgot about the rolls' rich flavor, even after moving away from Cincinnati. Customers were quite happy when the Schnecken Club was introduced and had no difficulty qualifying for the program of "Buy 12, Get 1 free." As further testimony of their popularity, at least one Clifton realtor chose to serve schnecken at open houses, with reported good success.

Already known to be a favorite, after the full line retail shop bakery closed in 2000, the production of this cherished item did not cease entirely. The love of schnecken became quite apparent during holiday seasons, as people who were unable to get to the store themselves had family members, neighbors and co-workers rush to the store on "schnecken runs" to buy as many loaves as were permitted. Needless to say, after Tom and Moe switched their operation to only making wedding cakes, those fans lucky enough to be on Ludlow Avenue at the right time were thrilled with the occasional unscheduled sighting of the sandwich board sign that announced, "Schnecken Today!"

"The schnecken beckons," a phrase coined by Brad Thie, Ron's son, perfectly describes the essence of schnecken cravings. Tom says schnecken are comfort food, a fact confirmed by many customers. One couple, delayed on departure of their honeymoon because of car trouble, drowned their sorrows by eating a loaf of schnecken on a park bench by Burnet Woods. Whatever the reason, many people developed a true addiction, even to the point of going into schnecken withdrawal when none was available.

Joyzell George shared that while pregnant with her son, she *needed* a schnecken. The only problem was that the bakery had closed for vacation. After she got home, she opened the Yellow Pages and proceeded to call every bakery in the phone book to see if they had schnecken. Because they weren't sure what she was asking for, she had to keep describing what it was. She tried to tell them about the dough, the butter as it runs down your fingers when it is warm, the raisins, the cinnamon, the texture and the taste. She was unsuccessful and very disappointed. Joyzell related that she once made a choice not to use the cash she had with her for the bus, but rather to buy a piece of schnecken. She will tell you the walk home was a long one, but she felt her decision was well worth the price. On another occasion, after entering the bakery and taking her number, she went to the display case and "picked out" the schnecken that she wanted. Unfortunately, someone else was ahead of her. So there she was, assessing the next best looking one, when the bakers brought out a new batch. She got to pick from that freshly baked group, and instead of buying just one, she bought three. A happy day, indeed.

Tom tells one of his favorite stories about a customer who came in for low-fat products after a visit to her cardiologist. She had been told her cholesterol levels were elevated and she should try to incorporate more whole grains in her diet. She inquired about the oat bran muffins, and Tom let her know there were some that would be out of the oven and available in about twenty minutes if she could wait, but she didn't have time. She then asked about the bran muffins, and he politely told her they'd be out in about ten minutes. In her frustration, the exasperated woman said, "What the heck, give me a schnecken." She had tried to behave herself…

One of the amazing stories about schnecken cravings, recounted more than once, was shared by a former shop worker. A gentleman came into the bakery one day and ordered a loaf of schnecken. He then proceeded to sit down at a table in the front of the store and eat the entire loaf! Knowing that schnecken is jam packed with butter, all of the girls in the storefront teased that they should have 911 on call. Happily, they saw him many times after that in the bakery.

Strong yearnings for the taste of schnecken were especially intense during the holidays. Many of the Virginia Bakery customers say nothing could compare to the taste of schnecken warm from the oven and made the pastry a part of all their family traditions. These folks made sure to order schnecken and were willing to stand in line starting at as early as five o'clock in the morning (even in the freezing cold) to get as many schnecken as they could for their own celebrations and to give as gifts to people near and far. Family members living out of town anticipated the welcome gifts, sometimes reporting that they had been devoured in less than an hour. Even if extra were sent to be stored in the freezer, they seldom lasted more than a few weeks.

From the employees' perspective, schnecken, especially during the holidays, created a tremendous workload, a crowded workspace (with schnecken stored and stacked high on every available surface and hallway) and a chance to observe some interesting human behavior. The desire for schnecken, as well as all the baked goods that "flew off the shelves," actually caused altercations to break out between customers when those who had been waiting for their turn would observe someone ahead of them buy out all the remaining loaves. The demand was tremendous, so much so that one man was successful, during peak seasons, in buying schnecken for $6.50 each and selling them to people who didn't want to deal with the crowds in the shop for $10.00 in the parking lot.

During the middle of the day, a common occurrence was for Tom to inform Moe that only about two hundred schnecken remained, which meant someone would have to walk up the street, counting off people and informing them that depending on how many they each planned to buy, the cakes would run out quickly. The employee said to anyone in line beyond number fifty, "Sorry, it doesn't look good; but we'll be open again tomorrow at 7:00 a.m.," and then hoped the crowd wasn't going to turn surly.

On one occasion, 7:00 a.m. wasn't early enough. Tom still laughs as he tells the story about two men, schnecken fanatics, who had come to the bakery because they absolutely had to have some schnecken, only to be told that the supply had run out and none was available that afternoon. They asked when the bakers would be making more, and Tom told them "all night." They asked if they could come under cover of darkness and get fifty loaves. Tom jokingly told them yes and they should wear trench coats and dark glasses. Sure enough, at 5:00 a.m. when Tom happened to step out on the back steps for a smoke, a long black car rolled up, parked across the street under the gaslight, flashed its lights and then went silent. Two men in trench coats and dark glasses emerged and approached the back door. One of them fleetingly displayed an "FBI" badge and said, "We're here for the schnecken, Sir. Just the schnecken." Needless to say, this event stirred things up in the back shop that morning.

Envision a day when the bakers had spent all morning, from just after midnight onward on December 23, making schnecken for the eager customers. As the crowd groaned in expectation, Tom looked in the oven to see how much longer. Something was wrong. The schnecken was pale and puffing out of the molds. He quickly pulled one strap of pans out of the oven and pinched off a piece of dough. (The schnecken pans had slots on the sides in order to attach them to one another. This way, a group of five went in the oven as one piece, making placing them into and pulling them out of the oven more efficient.) The taste quickly told him there was no salt in the dough. Five men had been working four hours making $1,500 worth of schnecken that this "soon to know and become angry" group would most likely have gladly thrown at them while still hot from the oven. (The bakers called hot schnecken "kitchen napalm" because it can stick to you and burn like the dickens.) This "bad day" event did, in fact, happen and could have been avoided if the person who had the job of mixing had tasted the dough like he was supposed to do. Tom's message: "Don't be afraid to use all your senses: it's the really cool part of baking, the Zen of baking." With hundreds of people still wanting their schnecken, the back shop men started over, staying there and baking until the job was done. The bakers got out of kitchen around 7:00 p.m. after putting in a fourteen-hour day. The Thies stayed later to accommodate customers who, in preparation of going out of town, were still coming to pick up their orders until almost 10:00 p.m. that night.

Holidays brought in people whom the employees might not see regularly but who stopped in when they came back to town. Some people would call and try to bribe Moe to put some schnecken aside for them. A couple of times Moe told someone she knew and had liked forever and who was practically in tears to meet her on Hosea Avenue and then she'd stash some in their car. She sometimes imagined she needed a black trench coat to wear when meeting the people under the gaslight on a foggy night. If Tom knew she was doing that, he never said anything; or maybe he thought, "Good for her, and I'm going to stay out of it."

Some really tall tales were fabricated by desperate customers in order to get their schnecken and dinner rolls at the last minute because they hadn't called ahead. One time, Moe felt really bad that an order that had been placed was not filled. She began to question the truthfulness of the situation when that identical excuse kept coming year after year by the same person. That's when she began hiding some throughout the building. The plan was successful—only once did she forget about a hiding place and found a "furry" schnecken in April.

The bakery had so many orders for schnecken during the holiday season that one of the upstairs apartments was turned into schnecken headquarters. Part-time workers came on board during the holiday season, hired and trained for the sole purpose of artfully wrapping the loaves in thick wax paper and securely packing them in the specially designed white rectangular boxes with the Virginia Bakery's trademark red lettering and red-and-white twisted string. These "schnecken angels," as they became known over time, came in before dawn to do this work in preparation for shipping them across the United States. Thousands of them were mailed to the southern states and out west to California, as well as all over the world, including such places as Hawaii, England, Canada and Mexico.

In the final years, Virginia Bakery sold nearly ten thousand of the golden brick loaves during the holiday season, shipping over seven thousand schnecken as Christmas gifts. Initially, boxes would be packed and run down to UPS daily; in the later years, a UPS truck was sent directly to the bakery for daily routine pickups.

Bill Thie, Tom's grandfather, taught him the initial steps of how to make schnecken; the complete responsibility was not ever given to many employees. The first job Tom learned, at the age of twelve, was to pat schnecken butter into the pans, for which he was paid seventy-five cents an hour.

In the bakery, the process of making schnecken began with mixing the dough, then an overnight resting period, followed by intensive work, such as rolling out ten-foot-long ropes of dough by hand on the bakery's long, smooth wooden table versus using a sheeter machine commonly used in most modern bakery operations. According to Tom, a decent baker should be able to roll a full piece of schnecken, which makes twenty loaves, in less than twenty minutes. This step was followed by an hour-long proof and fifty-five minutes in the oven. Then they needed to cool before being wrapped. The amazing thing is that Virginia Bakery made several batches of them daily throughout the year. With regularity, the bakers made about 250 pounds of yellow dough at a time, taking extreme care not to tear the dough when rolling it. On a good day, at full speed, Virginia Bakery could make and box 360 schnecken.

Once the dough was prepared and sliced, the rolls were put into the five-strap pans and allowed to proof once more. The individual schnecken molds were a slightly different size than we are generally able to buy now—smaller and deeper than most bread loaf pans and made of a thicker, heavier metal.

After coming out of the oven, the schnecken pans were left to sit for a few minutes before the loaves were flipped out onto sheet pans on the "dump rack." The emptied molds were filled back up with "schnecken butter" so that the thick glaze stayed in them, new dough was added and the process of proofing and baking was repeated. Only after every fifth baking were the pans washed in hot water only, no soap. Just like a favorite cast-iron skillet, the schnecken molds needed to be kept in a seasoned condition to ensure that the schnecken wouldn't stick. Some of the family members think that the bakery's great big oven also made a significant difference in the taste.

Ron remembers seeing his dad, Bill, walk by and, with his bare finger, touch the hot schnecken molds right out of the oven because a critical part of a good schnecken is knowing the correct moment to take them out of their pans. If they were "dumped out" right away, straight from the oven, all the brown gooey stuff would run off. If they waited too long, a hammer and chisel would have been needed to get them out. When feeling the baked dough with his palm, his dad would know when the moment was right. He'd take his apron to protect his hands, grab hold of the pans and flip them over, turning out loaves as pretty as could be. Howard and Tom, in succession, as well as some of the other trained bakers, learned this same essential technique.

Breaking down recipes from commercial size to home kitchen amounts is difficult, and Tom found that the schnecken recipe was especially tricky to convert. He faced numerous challenges and went through various stages and multiple attempts before being able to create a manageable size. Sometimes, while trying to adjust for the more common-sized pans available, he added more to the pan only to find that doing so caused butter to run out into the oven. The first time he made the home kitchen–sized version, the oven caught on fire. He's worked the snags out now, and the result tastes superb.

In the past, whenever people would ask for the schnecken recipe, the Thie bakers would just point to their heads and smile. The recipe for their popular pastry has always been a closely guarded secret, with a couple of exceptions. During the exploratory phase of this book, one story was provided that suggested Bill had been willing to share the recipe under special circumstances.

The story was shared by the daughter of one of Virginia Bakery's previous bakers. He worked for them for seven years and then went on to open his own successful bakery (Schwegmann's Bakery), which was "due in part to the kind, generous teaching and support from the Thies." Although Bill was known for *never* giving out that recipe, in this instance, he had allowed the baker to make schnecken because the bakery wouldn't be near Clifton.

The most recent sharing of the commercial-sized recipe took place one year after the Virginia Bakery had permanently closed its doors. In 2006, after Paige Busken talked with him at the bakery's closing auction, Tom decided to lease the famous schnecken recipe to Busken Bakery, another Cincinnati family-operated bakery, so that they could make and sell one of Virginia Bakery's signature products. In November of that year, billboard signs announced "Schtock up on Schnecken," and as Busken Bakery advertised, families were once again able to enhance their holidays one delicious slice after another.

And now the recipe is being shared just one more time. Because of Tom's adaptation work, you, the reader, have access to the secret that was closely guarded for at least four generations. With the home cook's version of this renowned recipe, you have the ability to make schnecken any time you feel the craving.

SCHNECKEN

This recipe requires a 12 oz. piece of yellow dough (see page 109).
Yield: one schnecken.

Prepare an 8" x 4" (as deep as you can find) pan by lightly greasing or spraying the mold with a vegetable shortening before you put the "schnecken butter" in the baking pan. Doing so prevents sticking and helps release the cake in the end.

Schnecken Butter
3 oz. unsalted butter
3 oz. margarine

Mix together and spread evenly over the bottom of the 8" x 4" schnecken pan.

You can adjust the 6 ounces of butter mix to make the rolls gooier or drier as you prefer. However, don't skimp on the melted butter (below) used on the inside to wash the dough prior to the sugar.

At the bakery there was no need to grease the pans as the molds were well seasoned, but at home I find doing so to be helpful. We only washed the molds after every five times they were in the oven and only used very hot water. Don't wash your schnecken pans with soap. This way they will stay seasoned and the schnecken will be less likely to stick.

The Schnecken

3 Tbs. melted butter

12 oz. yellow dough

½ cup + 1 Tbs. sugar

¼ tsp. cinnamon

1 Tbs. Raisins—for plump, juicy raisins, soak them in water for several hours or overnight

Egg wash—whisk one whole egg, add an equal amount water and whisk again

Flour your table and dough.

Roll dough into a rectangle about 4" x 18"

Dust off the flour from both sides and gently re-roll. Try to get corners square.

Wash bottom 1" edge of dough lightly with egg wash and remainder of dough with the melted butter.

Combine cinnamon and sugar and spread evenly over buttered portion of dough only. Scatter raisins over same.

Roll up schnecken toward you, starting with the 4" top side, and seal with egg wash at the bottom. Try to keep the roll tight and the edges straight. If you stretch the dough away from you and then roll it, your roll will come out tighter. Cut the roll into three equal pieces and place in buttered mold, with spiraled cut side up.

Let proof in a warm place until ready to bake. The rolls will double in size and fill out the pan. There are many variables, but you can expect at least forty-five minutes.

Dough should always be covered and not exposed to open air when proofing in order to avoid having a "skin" develop, which can cause ugly blotches on your finished product.

I prefer to proof schnecken by covering the dough with a cloth in a warm area of the room (versus a low-temperature oven) because it doesn't melt the butter in the bottom of the mold before baking. I don't know if this makes the schnecken better, but that's the way I do it.

Preheat oven to 375 degrees.

Place the schnecken pan on a cookie sheet to catch excess butter in the center of upper rack and bake for a total of forty-five minutes.

While normally you should not open the oven door while something is baking, you will need to break that open door policy here. After about twenty minutes, open the door and flatten the surface of the schnecken with a spatula. Gently press the dough back in the pan, being careful not to force the butter out of the mold. You may need to do this again, right at the end of the baking time (at about the thirty-five- to forty-minute mark), but if your schnecken looks flat on top, skip this second step.

When schnecken are golden brown on top, they're done. However, you can bake them how you like. Preferences run the gamut from almost raw to dry and dark.

Let the schnecken rest for five minutes in order for the buttery goo to absorb into the dough.

Turn them out of the pan and use all of your willpower to let them cool before you eat them. Good luck!

Note from Cynthia:

As a lifelong customer and connoisseur of Virginia Bakery products and their flavors, as well as a researcher for this book, I was very aware of the importance the Thies placed on using fresh, natural ingredients, such as real butter. For this reason, I was surprised to find margarine listed as one of the ingredients in making schnecken. After questioning Tom about this, the following schnecken history unfolded.

The recipe Tom is providing is factually based on the recipe he has known and used for the past twenty-some years. Although conjecture, because his father has passed away, we believe we have pieced together the evolution of the margarine's inclusion.

Back in the late 1890s and at the turn of the twentieth century, margarine was not a commonly used item, so it is fair to assume that no baked goods produced by Wilhelm Frederick Thie had margarine in them.

From multiple stories that have been handed down, as well as firsthand information provided by people who worked alongside him, there is absolutely no doubt that Bill Thie believed in using nothing but quality ingredients and that he had a strong dislike for margarine. The idea of his having used margarine in any of his products is very unlikely and hard to believe.

So it is most likely that sometime after 1976 Howard, being influenced by the media and scientific findings of that period, believed that margarine was the healthier choice and adjusted the recipe so that it would be better for his customers. However, in order to keep the buttery flavor that Virginia Bakery customers had come to expect, he continued to use half fresh butter in the "schnecken butter." Tom, picking up where his father left off, continued to use the recipe as it had been handed down to him.

More recent studies are bringing concerns to light about the use of margarine, and we now "know" that Tom's grandfather was right and butter was the better choice. Luckily, Virginia Bakery kept real, fresh butter in all of its recipes. Up until the time the bakery closed, Jim Eberle, of Eberle & Sons, remarked, "You guys use more butter than all the rest of the bakeries combined." This full-service food supplier was on Beekman Street, and during the Christmas season, the owners would let Virginia Bakery store schnecken in their freezer, which was two stories high and about fifty feet by fifty feet—big enough to drive a forklift around in it—just the right place for thousands of schnecken!

For anyone who wants to experiment and go back in time to what the 1927 recipe contained, Tom suggests the following, but be aware that doing so is making a change in the recipe you've become accustomed to and loved.

> The schnecken recipe provided is the version I learned from my father and used in the bakery and contains margarine in the schnecken butter pan dressing. With what I now know about margarine, I prefer to use half salted butter and half unsalted butter in my pan dressing.

Coffee Cakes

In 1950, Clementine Paddleford, a visiting food editor for *This Week* (a *Cincinnati Enquirer* supplement), stepped into a downtown taxi and told the driver she wanted to visit Virginia Bakery. Before she had a chance to give the man the address, he took off on their way. When she asked him about his knowing the directions, he replied that everybody in town knew that Virginia Bakery was near the corner of Clifton and Ludlow and added, "Folks go there from all over just to get the Thies' coffee cakes." As Hattie explained to Willard Clopton in 1961 for his *Cincinnati Post and Times Star* article, "People's tastes don't change…This is a German town still. Coffee cake's the big seller, as always." Coffee cakes were the favorite Virginia Bakery items for some of the Thie family members, too, and there were plenty to choose from. As reported in the *Bakery*'s "Cincinnati Bakery Tour," Virginia Bakery's product list included "80 types of coffee cakes."

Polk Laffoon IV, in his April 22, 1977 article in the *Cincinnati Post*, reported about the early days: "With only his mother to help and a block of ice to keep the milk cold, [Bill] began turning out coffee cakes and bread that some breakfast aficionados still say is the *sine qua non* of a civilized awakening." Over the years, as the bakery grew, Bill took care to let people know about them. In the 1960 General Mills "Vitality News" Merchandising Feature, Bill shared that he advertised a special item once a week in the Cincinnati newspapers. He felt that doing so not only resulted in large sales of the coffee cake or other item featured but also brought additional business for other baked goods. Bill warned that bakeries couldn't expect dramatic sales

Name Gains National Fame!

Streusel-topped coffee cakes *landed the Virginia Bakery, Cincinnati, Ohio, in This Week's food feature by Clementine Paddleford. Above, Mrs. Thie and sons, Wm., left, and Carl, inspect the product they've made famous.*

Photographed by Norman Gordon. Courtesy of Black Star.

results from "one-shot" ads; rather, advertising and public relations required ongoing efforts.

Fresh coffee cakes for breakfast were always a treat, but they were equally welcomed by many customers for dessert. And if there were any leftover goodies, warming them up in the oven for breakfast the next day was also something special. Over the course of conversations with former customers, at one time or another every baked good was mentioned. However, there seem to have been two front runners in this category: the cinnamon crumb and the double butter. Everyone seemed to feel that nobody to this day makes a cinnamon crumb cake the way Virginia Bakery did. Numerous people shared that their families had a standing order that included a weekly cinnamon crumb cake, pointing out that the large, chunky cinnamon crumb streusel topping was excellent and that the occasional dips in the dough that ended up holding more of the streusel were prized bites. As for the butter cakes, again the consensus was that no other bakery has perfected a double butter that could match the Thies'. Theirs were described as incredible, with deep wells filled with the delectable taste of real butter. Some folks mentioned that just sharing the memories of this family favorite made their mouths water.

The coffee cakes covered with real fruit were also delicious. Comments included that the apricot and peach were good; the cherry was a favorite and quite attractive on a Christmas brunch table; and the apple was very popular with thin slices of fruit nicely arranged in rows, as were the open-faced fresh prune plum cakes during the season they were available in Cincinnati. They were something that couldn't be found anywhere else. Annie Glenn remembered, "Customers loved plum cake season."

In addition, customers had a wide variety of Danish coffee cakes from which to choose, including tea rings, both plain and filled with a cinnamon-nut mixture; roll-ins, fruit and almond; and pockets, buttercream, cheese and fruit filled. Jerry Armstead remembered how they had to roll out the Danish dough, fill it with butter, set it back in the refrigerator and then get it out and roll it again several times before all the ingredients were blended correctly to get the desired flakiness. Bill Pritz commented that Virginia Bakery had items, such as the tea rings and some of these other Danish products, that aren't often found in bakeries anymore. He added that the way the bakers made one thing out of another made the process interesting. Leftover pastry was not thrown away. Instead, it was put to good use—actually recycled, using the current term—by remixing with other ingredients to make different cakes and fillings. There was no waste; everything was utilized.

Mother doughs, such as the yellow dough and Danish, were doughs that were the basis for many items. With slight variations, such as substituting honey for sugar or adding different fillings, the bakers were able to make a variety of baked goods all stemming from one original recipe. In the bakery, the use of one dough for several coffee cakes created an underlying unity to the variety. Bill Pritz felt that gave a certain integrity to their work. "Component ingredients would be mixed different ways to create the variations on one thing and the ability to discriminate, such as butter and double butter cakes, or cinnamon rolls and double cinnamon rolls. They were in essence the same thing really but for people who wanted more of the streusel or filling."

Although many customers would not have thought to ask, especially during the eras when people weren't so consumed with the idea of magazine-cover-thin figures, some shared that they were able to buy half of a coffee cake. This was a service undoubtedly appreciated by those who lived alone and didn't need a family-sized item or were attempting to maintain their waistlines while gratifying their gustatory desires.

A few people mentioned that what they liked about Virginia Bakery coffee cakes and Danish products was the use of pecans or walnuts, not the less expensive nuts like some other bakeries used. They were expensive, even by today's standard: Bill Thie mentioned in 1977 that due to a shortage, pecans were like gold, almost forty dollars per pound.

The recipe for the yellow dough below is the beginning of all the coffee cakes on the following pages. The recipe for the Danish dough on page 119 precedes all the Danish coffee cakes.

Yellow Dough

Sponge:
2 cups warm water
3 packs instant dry yeast
3 cups all-purpose flour

Start yeast in warm water for 5 minutes, or until bloomed. Add flour, mix well. Cover bowl with a cloth and let rise until it doubles or the sponge starts to fall. Depending on the temperature, this could take 1 to 2 hours.

Add:
$1\frac{1}{4}$ cup sugar
4 tsp. salt
1 cup vegetable shortening
4 oz. salted butter (1 stick) softened to room temperature
$\frac{1}{2}$ cup egg yolks
1 cup cool milk
1 cup cool water
9 (approximately) cups flour—preferably 3 cups winter flour (pastry flour) and 6 cups all-purpose flour

Mix all ingredients to form a soft dough, which should be quite sticky—soft, pliable and moist—but not batter like. If the dough forms a tight ball, you've added too much flour. Add a little water.
Yield: a little over $6\frac{1}{2}$ pounds

The winter flour helps to soften the dough and gives the yellow dough a better texture. Not essential, but nice to have. All-purpose flour will produce perfectly fine results.

Starting the dough early in the day or a day ahead is best. Fresh yellow dough is difficult to work with. I recommend refrigerating the dough, allowing it to stiffen. Measured pieces can be wrapped separately. For coffee cakes, such as the cinnamon crumb, as well as schnecken, divide dough into nine pieces. Each piece will weigh approximately twelve ounces. Some other recipes, such as the Hungarian Bundt, will call for two twelve-ounce pieces.

The dough takes a few hours to rise after being in the refrigerator overnight. The sponge method is not a quick way to make bakery goods, but the result is worth the wait. The dough is easy to work with.

If you're going to use the divided dough soon, you can just put it on a floured tray and cover with a towel. If the dough will be frozen for future use, put it in plastic bags. The refrigerated dough should be used within forty-eight hours; the frozen can be kept for up to a month. The yeast activity will decline rapidly after a month and your dough will be flat. When making an item from frozen dough, simply thaw it in the refrigerator or in the microwave on defrost.

CINNAMON CRUMB COFFEE CAKE

This cake requires a 12-oz. piece of yellow dough (see page 109) and cinnamon crumbs (see page 139). Yield: one cake

Spread dough evenly over the bottom of a well greased 8" x 8" pan. Pat to flatten with no lip.
Wash the dough with melted butter and cover generously with cinnamon crumbs.

The topping recipe yields enough to cover two cakes with a layer of cinnamon crumb streusel as they were made in the bakery.

Those of you who enjoy a really thick layer of the cinnamon crumbs can benefit from what Cynthia calls her happy accident (of misreading the recipe during a test baking) and use the whole mixture on top of one coffee cake.

Often a customer would ask to have the cake covered with sifted powdered sugar.

After putting crumbs on the dough in the baking pan, let the cake rise in a warm place until dough is almost doubled.
Preheat oven to 375 degrees.
Place pan in the center of upper rack and bake for 20–25 minutes—until cake springs back when tested.
Cakes are easier to remove from pan when slightly warm.

BUTTER COFFEE CAKE

This cake requires a 12-oz. piece of yellow dough (see page 109) and buttercream filling (see page 138).
Yield: one cake

Spread dough evenly over the bottom of a well-greased 8" x 8" pan. Flatten with fingertips, being careful not to make any holes that would allow the buttercream to get under the dough.
Creating a small, thin rim by pulling the edges up the sides of the pan to form a lip is also crucial in order to contain the buttercream so the filling doesn't run under the dough.

When I would teach the new guys, it was common for them to press too hard with their fingertips, leaving little depressions and an uneven dough. As the cake would bake, the melted buttercream would flow into these holes and create puddles surrounded by hills of dough. The result in such cases is one bite dough, next bite buttercream. You want both in the same bite. The pools or puddles of butter cream are a result of the dough not being spread evenly over the bottom of the pan. So, strive to keep your dough even. As for the lip, I like to keep it as thin as possible and about one inch up the side of the pan so you don't get a big hunk of dough in the last bite of each slice.

Using up to 1½ cups of buttercream for a double butter, spread evenly over the dough with a spatula. If you prefer making a single butter, use about a cup of the buttercream. Let the pan set in a warm place until dough rises—almost doubles.

Preheat oven to 350 degrees.

Place pan in the center of upper rack and bake in oven until desired doneness—approximately 20–30 minutes.

Let cool slightly on a rack, then remove.

The butter cakes are actually easier to remove when slightly warm.

The double butter used to get a dot of powdered sugar in the center so the store girls could tell them apart.

WINKY DINK COFFEE CAKE

Follow the directions for the butter cake, using a mixture of 1 cup of buttercream, ½ cup of shredded coconut, and ½ cup pineapple puree as the topping. (You can puree drained canned pineapple in a blender or food processor.)

> This got a cherry in the middle for identification.

OLD-FASHIONED CINNAMON COFFEE CAKE

This cake requires a 12-oz. piece of yellow dough (see page 109).
Additional ingredients needed: butter, granulated sugar, powdered sugar and cinnamon.
Yield: one cake

Spread dough evenly over the bottom of a well-greased 8" x 8" pan. Pat to flatten with no lip.

You need sixteen pieces of firm butter about the size of a piece of popcorn or a Hershey's kiss (a slightly rounded teaspoon each). Place them—evenly distributed—in a 4x4 pattern. Press them into but not through the dough. You want to avoid allowing/having the butter get under the dough.

Sprinkle the entire cake surface with approximately ½ cup of a cinnamon sugar mixture, made from ½ cup of sugar and ½ tsp. of cinnamon. Cover this with ½ cup of powdered sugar.

> Here's where personal taste comes into play. I believe a spice should say something like "cinnamon," not "CINNAMON!" I like to know the spice is there, but it should never overpower. Therefore, I tend to make my cinnamon sugar on the light side. Others may prefer more.

> This cake is drier than the buttercream, so don't expect it to be real gooey.

Actually, the cake looks better if just a few spots of cinnamon sugar show through.

After putting the sugar toppings on the dough, let the cake rise in a warm place until dough is almost doubled.

Preheat oven to 375 degrees.

Bake for 20 to 25 minutes—until cake springs back when tested.

Cakes are easier to remove from pan when slightly warm.

PRALINE PECAN COFFEE CAKE

Follow the directions for the Old-fashioned Cinnamon, replacing the two sugars with the following topping.

Mix equal parts light brown sugar and whole pecans—½ cup each. Moisten slightly with 2 Tbs. of melted butter. Sprinkle mixture over entire surface of cake. .

FRESH APPLE COFFEE CAKE

This cake requires a 12-oz. piece of yellow dough (see page 109) and Granny Smith apples.

Additional ingredients needed: powdered sugar, granulated sugar and cinnamon.

Yield: one cake

Spread dough evenly over the bottom of a well-greased 8" x 8" pan. Flatten with fingertips, being careful not to make any holes that would allow the fruit juices to get under the dough.

Creating a small, thin rim by pulling the edges up the sides of the pan to form a lip is also very important in order to contain the fruit juices so they don't run under the dough.

Strive to keep your dough even. Make the lip as thin as possible and about one inch up the side of the pan so you don't get a big hunk of dough in the last bite of each slice. (See photo on page 111.)

Prepare the fruit. The Granny Smith apples (approximately 2) need to be cored, peeled and sliced into thin wedges (approximately ¼" thick).

Arrange the fruit by shingling or overlapping the fruit in single rows with the round side up. Usually three rows of apples work. Sometimes you have to fill in the gaps with bits and pieces of apples.

Let the cakes proof about 20 minutes until almost doubled.

Prior to baking, the cakes are dusted with a sugar mixture: combine 2 Tbs. of powdered sugar, 2 Tbs. of granular sugar and ¼ tsp. of cinnamon and sprinkle over the fruit.

Preheat the oven to 375 degrees.

Place pan in the center of upper rack and bake the cake for 30 to 40 minutes until the edges turn brown.

FRESH PLUM COFFEE CAKE

Follow the directions for fresh apple coffee cake, except replace the apple slices with prune plums (approximately eight) that have been split in half and had the pits removed. Usually four rows of plum halves, cut side up, cover the top in a single layer.

Combine 2 Tbs. of powdered sugar and 2 Tbs. of granular sugar. Prior to baking, dust the arranged fruit on top of the cake with the sugar mixture.

HUNGARIAN BUNDT Á LA WILL DAWSON

This cake requires 1½ pounds (two of the 12-oz. pieces) of yellow dough (see page 109), schnecken goo (see page 142), cinnamon sugar (see page 140) and roll icing (see page 142).

Yield: one cake

> This Hungarian Bundt is one of my favorites. It was the job of the doughnut man to make these every Thursday. My favorite doughnut man was Will Dawson. Will was about ten years younger than my dad, had been in the Korean War, was a professional chaurcutier (sausage maker), one of the best cooks I know (his fried chicken from the doughnut fryer was to die for—we still talk about it) and the most loyal man I know. He was there *every* morning at 1:00 a.m. to open the bakery. He lit the ovens, pulled the doughs and made sure we had fresh coffee at 4:00 a.m. I thanked the Lord often for Will Dawson. Oh, and I forgot to mention, he was a hell of a baker too!

Making the Hungarian Bundt was more of a process than a recipe. Will made 12 at a time. To make one Bundt, bear with me.

Prepare a bowl with a ½ vegetable oil and ½ melted butter mixture—about a cup each should do for our purpose.

Set up a drain rack or a rack on a sheet pan.

Prepare a bowl full of cinnamon sugar—about 2 cups.

Prepare the Bundt mold by greasing well a 9" round Bundt or tube mold.

With a pastry bag, pipe a tube of schnecken goo (approximately 1 cup) around the bottom of the mold.

To assemble the Bundt, take the 1½ pounds of yellow dough and divide it into 12 pieces. Each piece will weigh approximately 2 ounces.

With your cupped hand, roll the pieces into little balls.

Place the balls in the oil/butter mix and coat.

Remove the balls and allow to drain on the rack about ten seconds.

Roll the balls in the cinnamon sugar mixture.

Place the balls side by side in the mold on top of the piped schnecken goo.

Let proof about ½ hour or until doubled.

Preheat oven to 375 degrees.

Place pan in the center of upper rack and bake for 30 to 40 minutes or until golden.

Let the mold rest about 5 minutes and then turn over onto a plate.

This is easy to do at home. Put the plate upside down on top of the Bundt mold and turn the whole thing over. Remove the mold and stare in amazement. You've just made the best Bundt cake ever.

> Be careful when handling straight from the oven—this part is a lot like schnecken. Watch out, the hot goo really burns.
>
> Okay! I'm gonna let you break the "don't eat while hot" rule on this one. Dig in!

While the Bundt is still warm, smear the top with the roll icing. As it melts, it will form a glaze running over the sides.

LEAF LOAF

This cake requires a one-pound (16-oz.) piece of yellow dough (see page 109), buttercream filling (see page 138) and yellow crumbs (see page 144).
Yield: one loaf

On a floured surface, roll the dough into a rectangle about 18" high and 9" wide. Brush off any excess flour.

Cover the dough with a thin layer of buttercream filling—approximately 1 cup.

Sprinkle with yellow crumbs—approximately 1 cup.

Some people like roll icing drizzled across the top and sides of these breads; some like it with powdered sugar; some just plain.

Like a scroll, roll the top down and the bottom up so they meet in the middle. Place the rolled-up dough (with seam side up) in a well-greased small (8" x 4") bread mold.

Brush the top lightly with egg wash and cover with an additional cup of yellow crumbs.

Proof until almost doubled and filling the bread pan.

Preheat oven to 375 degrees.

Place pan in the center of upper rack and bake for 45 to 55 minutes until the top starts to brown.

Remove from pan and cool on rack.

GRANDMA'S BREAD

This cake requires a one-pound (16-oz.) piece of yellow dough (see page 109), tea ring filling (see page 143) and cinnamon crumbs (see page 139).
Yield: one loaf

Follow the directions as written above for the leaf loaf with the following substitution:

Brush the rolled-out dough with melted butter and cover with approximately 2 cups of tea ring filling. Roll up like a scroll and place in the mold. After brushing the top lightly with egg wash, cover with 1 cup of cinnamon crumbs.

You can use the cake test to test theseloaves for doneness: if you press on the dough and it doesn't spring back, it's not done.

DANISH DOUGH

3 packets dry yeast
1 cup room temperature water
1 cup sugar
1½ tsp. salt
2 oz. (4 Tbs.) butter
2 oz. (4 Tbs.) shortening
¾ cup whole eggs
¼ cup egg yolks
1 cup refrigerated milk
1½ cups winter flour (if you are unable to find winter wheat, all purpose will work fine)
6 cups all-purpose flour
1 lb. butter

Bloom the yeast in the water.
Cream sugar, salt, butter and shortening in a mixer.
Add eggs and yolks, scrape and cream.
Add the yeast/water mixture and milk. Scrape and mix.
Add flour and mix until dough just comes together. You do not want to develop the gluten, so don't mix this too long.
Turn dough onto a floured half-sheet pan and refrigerate about half hour to firm dough.
Your final piece of dough will occupy half of this half-sheet pan when done. Try to keep that size in mind when rolling the dough—9" x 12".

Now we begin the roll-ins. You need 1 lb. of butter. (For those who prefer using some margarine, you can use half margarine/half butter. You need 1 lb. total of "roll in.")

As depicted in the diagram on page 120, this is the procedure.

The first roll: You're going to need some counter space. Roll the dough until it is approximately 27" wide by 12" tall.
Divide the dough visually into three pieces—each 9" wide by 12" tall.
Divide the butter that will be rolled in into 24 pieces.
On each of the two rectangles to the right (the center and far right sections), place 12 pieces of roll-in in a 3x4 pattern—3 across and 4 down.

Danish Roll-In

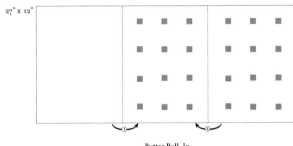

Butter Roll-In

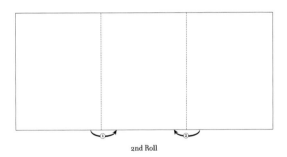

2nd Roll

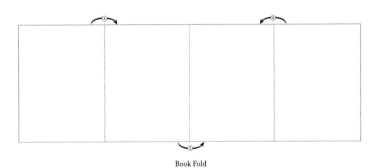

Book Fold

I insisted on rolling our own Danish dough. There is a huge difference, and the customers could tell. Making Danish by hand is a long, tedious process but well worth the effort. You can probably buy Danish dough from your baker, but if you've come this far you might as well go all the way and make your own. It really isn't that hard, but I can tell you, it was my least favorite day. We usually made about 150 pounds of Danish at a time. This small piece is easy.

The winter flour helps to soften the dough and gives a better texture. Not essential, but nice to have. All-purpose flour will produce perfectly fine results.

A few words about Danish dough: Danish gets it flakiness from two sources. The first is from the yeast. The second is from the butter trapped between the layers. There is a reason Danish is given the number and type of rolls it gets. Not enough layers and it's not flaky. Too many layers and the butter gets mixed into the dough and it will go flat. For the same reason, it is important to keep the dough cold so the butter stays firm and does not become mixed in the dough. Hence the much-needed refrigerator time. This was a real problem in a 100-degree bakery in the middle of summer. You had to move fast and wait a long time for the dough to cool. You want layers of fat trapped in between layers of dough. When the dough is baked, the water in the butter—yes, butter is 20 percent water—turns into steam. If properly trapped, the steam expands and creates little air pockets in the dough. So you get an initial pop from the yeast and an extra poof from the trapped steam. Pretty cool, huh?

You can store the dough wrapped for two days in the fridge or about a month in the freezer.

This dough can be divided into portions based on which recipes you're planning to make. This recipe yields eight 12-oz. portions or four 12-oz. portions plus three 16-oz. (1-lb.) portions.

Fold the unbuttered section on the left side over the center buttered section. Now fold the right side piece over the center.
You've just done your first tri-fold. Turn the piece one quarter turn, put the dough back on the pan and refrigerate for half hour.

Second roll: It gets easier. This is a simple tri-fold.

Roll the dough into the same 27" x 12" rectangle.

Fold the left third over the center and the right third over that. Turn the piece one quarter turn, put the dough back on the pan and refrigerate for half hour.

Third roll: This is the final roll, called a book fold or a four fold.

Roll the dough 36" x 12".

Draw a visual line down the center of the dough from top to bottom.

Fold the left edge to the center and now the right edge to the center. You now have two sections.

Fold one side over the other, like closing a book. Turn the piece one quarter turn and put the dough back on the pan. Refrigerate at least one hour before trying to use dough. Dough portions can be frozen.

Yield: 6 pounds

SEVEN SISTERS

This cake requires a 12-oz. piece of Danish dough (see page 119), buttercream filling (see page 138), yellow crumbs (see page 144), glaze (see page 142) and roll icing (see page 142).

Yield: 1 cake

Grease an 8" round cake pan well.

On a well-floured surface, roll the 12-oz. piece of Danish dough into a rectangle 12" tall by 6" wide.

Brush the flour off both sides.

Brush the bottom 1" edge with egg wash.

Spread a thin layer of buttercream (approximately ½ cup) on the remainder.

Cover the buttercream lightly with yellow crumbs (approximately ½ cup).

Roll from top down into a cylinder (which will be about 8" long).

Cut like a sushi roll into "seven honorable sisters."

Place the favorite sister, an end piece with cut side up, in the center and surround with her six siblings, also with cut sides up.

Wash the tops with egg wash and cover with ¾ cup yellow crumbs.

Proof, covered, in a warm area until doubled in size.

Preheat oven to 375 degrees.

Place pan in the center of upper rack and bake for approximately 30 minutes until golden brown.

When cool, remove from pan. The easiest way is to place a plate on top of the cake pan, turn the rolls over onto the plate and then flip them over again onto a second plate.

Glaze the top and drizzle with roll icing.

FRUIT POCKETS

This cake requires a 12-oz. piece of Danish dough (see page 119), fruit filling (see page 141), cinnamon crumbs (see page 139) or yellow crumbs (see page 144), glaze (see page 142) and roll icing (see page 142).

Yield: 1 cake

Grease an 8" x 8" coffee cake pan well.

On a well-floured surface, roll the 12-oz piece of Danish dough into a 12" x 12" square.

Brush the flour off the front and back of the dough.

Place the dough in the pan so the corners of the dough align with the center of each side of the pan. The corners of the dough will hang over the sides of the pan.

Make sure there is enough dough in the bottom of the pan to form a closed "pocket" when these corners are folded over. You don't want your filling running out the corners and under the dough. You'll see what I mean as we close the pocket.

Fill your pocket with your choice of fruit filling: apple, cherry or blueberry.

Fold the four corners of the dough to the center. The flaps should overlap and close up the pocket.

Brush the top lightly with egg wash and sprinkle with cinnamon crumbs or yellow crumbs. The apple pockets got cinnamon crumbs; the other fruit pockets got yellow crumbs.

Proof, covered, in a warm area for about 20 minutes.

Preheat oven to 375 degrees.

Place pan in the center of upper rack and bake for approximately 30 minutes until golden brown.

When cool, glaze and drizzle with roll icing.

> The pockets were the second thing an apprentice baker would tackle after learning the coffee cakes. Having learned how to handle yellow dough, which is really hard to mess up (you almost have to try), they were now ready to use a hand pin and learn about Danish dough.
>
> You need to use a lot of flour while working with the dough to keep it from sticking. You will brush it off when done, so be generous.

CHEESE POCKET

Follow directions on page 123, substituting cheese filling (see page 149), sprinkling cinnamon crumbs over the egg wash and dusting the cooled cake with powdered sugar instead of the roll icing.

BUTTERCREAM POCKET

Follow directions on page 123, substituting buttercream filling (see page 138), sprinkling cinnamon crumbs over the egg wash and dusting the cooled cake with powdered sugar instead of the roll icing.

COMBINATION POCKET

You can even combine ingredients: cherries and cheese or blueberries and buttercream.

FRUIT ROLL-IN

This cake requires a 12-oz. piece of Danish dough (see page 119), fruit filling (see page 141), yellow crumbs (see page 144), glaze (see page 142) and roll icing (see page 142).
Additional ingredients needed: almond paste
Yield: 1 cake

Grease an 8" round cake pan well.

On a well-floured surface, roll the 12-oz piece of Danish dough into a rectangle 8" tall by 15" wide.

Brush the flour off both sides.

Brush the bottom 1" edge with egg wash.

Spread a thin layer of almond paste (approximately ¾ cup) on the remainder.

Then add a thin layer of fruit filling (also approximately ¾ cup).

Roll from the top down and seal, creating a cylinder of dough about 15" long.

Bring the two ends together to form a circle and place in pan.

Proof, covered, in a warm area for approximately 20 minutes.

Following the circular path, cut down about halfway through the depth of circular cylinder of dough, being careful not to go through to the bottom.

Open dough to expose the insides.

Place a ring of fruit filling—approximately 1 cup—on top of the exposed area of dough.

Cover with yellow crumbs.

After the pockets, our novice baker moved on to the roll-ins. We only made cherry, blueberry and almond.

One thing you want to remember when rolling Danish is you are trying to maintain the layers of fat between the dough, so be gentle. You also want the dough to be cool, not still partially frozen or, worse, too warm.

Proof again until doubled.
Preheat oven to 375 degrees.
Place pan in the center of upper rack and bake for approximately 30 minutes
until golden brown.
When cool, glaze and drizzle with roll icing.

ALMOND ROLL-IN

Follow directions above, substituting more almond paste (approximately 1 ½
cup) for the fruit filling, making a thicker spread before the first proof and
adding an additional paste ring (approximately 1 cup) in the cut made after
the first proof.

PLAIN TEA RING

Four tea rings require a 3-lb. piece of
Danish dough (see page 119), cinnamon
sugar (see page 140), glaze (see page 142)
and roll icing (see page 142).

On a very large, well-floured surface, roll the
3-lb. piece of Danish dough into a rectangle
30" tall by 8" wide. The dough can hang
over the edge of your board or you could do
this sideways on a long counter.
Brush the flour off both sides.
Brush the top 1" edge with egg wash and
the remainder with melted butter.

Sprinkle cinnamon sugar over the butter.
Visually divide the dough into three pieces.
Fold the bottom third up over the middle third, and fold the top third down
over this. You now have three layers of dough with two layers of filling.
Lightly roll this rectangle to flatten dough.
Cut this piece into four equal strips from top to bottom.

Tea rings are a little difficult to do at home because it's hard to make just one. We usually made twelve at a time, which makes the dough easier to handle. You might want to consider making four at a time and freezing some for later baking. I'm going to tell you how to make four at a time. If you try to make just one, good luck.

The filled tea ring dough can also be used to make royals.

If you only want to bake one cake, this is the point where you should wrap the extra dough pieces securely and freeze.

Twist the strips like candy canes by holding one end in your left hand and rolling the other with your right. Bring the two ends together and seal to form a circle.

Turn the circle over and place on a greased or parchment-lined baking sheet. You will need two half-sheet pans to bake four tea rings—two cakes per pan.

Proof, covered, in a warm area until doubled in size.

Preheat oven to 375 degrees.

Place pan in the center of upper rack and bake for approximately 30 minutes until golden brown.

While still warm, wash with glaze and cover with roll icing.

FILLED TEA RING

These are made the same way as plain tea rings, except substitute tea ring filling (see page 143) in place of the cinnamon sugar. Be careful not to let the filling fall out when rolling up. After baking, while still slightly warm, glaze, coat with roll icing and top with pecan pieces.

ROYALS—APPLE, BLUEBERRY AND CHERRY

As with the tea rings, you will be working with a 12-oz. piece of Danish dough for each cake (see pages 126–127). This cake also requires fruit filling (see page 141), cinnamon or yellow crumbs (see pages 139 and 144), glaze (see page 142) and roll icing (see page 142).
Yield: 1 cake

Grease an 8" round cake pan well.

Take the piece of dough and prepare as you would for a filled tea ring.
Roll dough into long rope (about three feet long) and spiral around itself to form a flat disk.
Place the dough disk in the round pan and flatten to cover the whole bottom. Form a small lip around the edge to contain the fruit, much like the coffee cakes. (See photo on page 111.)

> At the bakery, the royals were made from the two outside edge strips of the tea ring dough. There was nothing wrong with them; the center pieces just made the prettiest tea rings.

Cover the entire cake with the fruit filling of your choice.

Put on the crumbs—cinnamon for apple, yellow for the other fruits. The crumbs were applied in a bulls-eye pattern with a dot in the middle and then the rest around the edges, leaving an exposed ring of fruit in the middle of these two.
Proof, covered, in a warm area until doubled in size.
Preheat oven to 375 degrees.
Place pan in the center of upper rack and bake for approximately 30 minutes until golden brown.
When done, remove from pan, glaze and drizzle fruit ring with roll icing.

Breakfast Rolls

Breakfast rolls were among the first items sold each morning and were, as reported in the "Cincinnati Bakery Tour" section of the February 1989 *Bakery* magazine, available in "more than 30 Danish and sweet roll varieties." Hours before the store opened, bakers were busy so that people could stop in on their way to work and make their mornings brighter with the aromas and tastes of fresh-from-the oven morsels. Others saved the treat for the weekend. Dick Nichols shared that Saturday meant sweet rolls and coffee: "I loved them!" Others apparently did also. Connie Lindsay shared a story about her husband and her father, who took turns "making a run" to Virginia Bakery in order to stock up for the family. When her father's turn came, he would place their order in her husband's car at work in Fairfield on his way back home. One day, her father called when he got back home to apologize that there had only been a few sweet rolls left at the bakery, so he sent three of them. Funny—there was only one in the box when her husband brought it into the house. Turns out they smelled so good in the car, her husband devoured them on the drive home. Warren Webster expressed his fondness for the cinnamon rolls because of the abundance of raisins in each one of them. "I suppose there is justification for these treats. I would consider the raisins as good antioxidants with which to offset what the schnecken, another favorite, was doing to me."

Just as the yellow dough used for the yeast coffee cakes was also turned into the sweet rolls, the Danish dough used for Danish coffee cakes was turned into delectable breakfast rolls too. For many folks, the flaky, scrumptious

Lou Dorsey making cinnamon rolls. *Provided by Caroline Seim. Courtesy of Howard Goldberg.*

pecan rolls were too tempting to resist, and they enjoyed the process of peeling away the layers, unwinding them as they ate the sticky buns. For the large majority of people, though, the favorite was butterscotch gems, as proven by the fact that Virginia Bakery sold dozens and dozens every day. Buying them right as they came out warm from the back shop, ready to be put in the display case, was a true pleasure—especially the ones in the center of the pan. All gem lovers considered them a real treat, thoroughly enjoying the bites that combined the brown sugar butterscotch crunch with the flakiness of Danish dough. Ron Thie admitted that because of working in the bakery he lost interest in most items, but he continued to love the pecan Danish items, including the butterscotch gems.

PLAIN SWEET DOUGH BREAKFAST ROLLS

The yeast breakfast rolls are easy to make.

These rolls require a 12-oz. piece of yellow dough (see page 109), cinnamon sugar (see page 140), glaze (see page 142) and roll icing (see page 142).
Yield: 6 rolls

Grease a half-sheet baking pan.

On a lightly floured surface, roll the 12-oz. piece of dough into a rectangle about 15" tall and 6" wide.
Brush the 6" bottom edge with egg wash.
Wash the rest of the dough piece with 2 Tbs. of melted butter and sprinkle with ¼ cup of cinnamon sugar.
Roll the dough from the top down, jelly roll fashion. Place seam on bottom.
Slice the dough cylinder evenly into six rolls.
Place the cut rolls, cut side up, on a greased baking sheet. Rolls should not touch—allow room for expansion.
Proof, covered, in a warm area until doubled in size.
Preheat oven to 375 degrees.
Place pan in the center of upper rack and bake for approximately 15 minutes until golden brown.
While still warm, glaze the rolls.
Then ice them with roll icing.

RAISIN ROLLS

These rolls require a 12-oz. piece of yellow dough (see page 109), cinnamon sugar (see page 140), raisins, glaze (see page 142) and roll icing (see page 142).
Yield: 6 rolls

These rolls are made the same way as the plain sweet dough rolls, with the addition of sprinkling ½ cup of raisins over the dough before rolling the cylinder shape.

CINNAMON ROLLS

These rolls require a 12-oz. piece of yellow dough (see page 109), cinnamon smear (see page 140), glaze (see page 142) and roll icing (see page 142).
Yield: 6 rolls

These rolls are made following the same method as the plain sweet dough rolls except the butter and cinnamon is replaced with a layer of cinnamon smear (approximately ½ cup).

DOUBLE CINNAMON ROLLS

These rolls require a 12-oz. piece of yellow dough (see page 109), cinnamon smear (see page 140), cinnamon crumbs (see page 139) and powdered sugar.
Yield: 6 rolls

These rolls are made the same way as the cinnamon rolls, with the addition of dipping the rolls in cinnamon crumbs after the rolls have been cut from the cylinder of dough so that the tops of the rolls will have a cover of crumbs. After the rolls come out of the oven, dust them with powdered sugar.

My favorite story about breakfast rolls involves a lot of alcohol and very little common sense. This happened while we were living above the bakery in one of the apartments. Living at work afforded the luxury of sleeping in until 4:00 a.m. One of the bakers' first duties was to prepare the breakfast rolls so they would be ready at 7:30 when the store opened. If they timed it right, the rolls would still be warm. As I came down the steps, I could hear the usual joking and clowning, slightly louder than usual. Entering the back shop, I found two of my best bakers drunk as skunks. The breakfast rolls were all made; however, they were all lined up in neat little rows on the bench. I said, "Good Morning guys. How do you think we're gonna get that bench in the oven?" They had forgotten to put the rolls on sheet pans. Funny. Hah, hah! Do them over.

PECAN ROLLS

These rolls require a 12-oz. piece of Danish dough (see page 119) and schnecken goo (see page 142).
Additional ingredients needed: cinnamon sugar (see page 140) and pecan pieces.
Yield: 6 rolls

> At the bakery, we piped the schnecken goo into pans with a pastry bag.
> At home, I just use my finger and a spoon. Less to clean. I like it clean, but I hate to clean, don't you?

Using a 6-muffin pan (or a dozen mold if you double the recipe), grease the cups well and place about 2 Tbs. of schnecken goo in the bottom of each muffin mold, followed by 2 Tbs. of pecan pieces in each cup.

On a well-floured surface, roll dough into a rectangle taller than wide—approximately 12" tall and 8" wide.
Brush bottom 1" edge with egg wash to seal and the remainder with 3 Tbs. of melted butter.
Sprinkle buttered portion with $\frac{1}{4}$ cup cinnamon sugar and $\frac{3}{4}$ cup pecan pieces.
Roll from top down and seal.
Cut the 12-oz. piece of dough into 6 pieces (or 12 pieces if doubling the recipe) and place them cut side up into the muffin cups.
Proof, covered, in a warm area until doubled in size.
Preheat oven to 375 degrees.
Place pan in the center of upper rack and bake for 25 to 30 minutes until golden brown.
Remove to rack and cool slightly.
While still warm, dump on pan and remove mold slowly. *Ohhh! Ahhh!*

PECAN CRISPS

These rolls require a 12-oz. piece of Danish dough (see page 119) and schnecken goo (see page 142).
Additional ingredients needed: cinnamon sugar (see page 140), pecan pieces and glaze (see page 142).
Yield: 6 rolls

Prepare the dough for crisps the same way as for pecan rolls.

After the dough has been cut into 6 pieces, sprinkle ½ cup of cinnamon sugar and 1 cup of pecan pieces on a work surface.

Use a small rolling stick (the size of a broom handle cut to a 15" to 18" length) to roll out the individual pieces in the mixture of cinnamon sugar and pecan pieces.

Turn over and roll dough several times, trying to embed the sugar and pecans into the dough.

Roll until each becomes a 6" disk.

Place the dough disks on a greased or parchment lined baking sheet.

Proof for about 15 minutes.

Preheat oven to 375 degrees.

Place pan in the center of upper rack and bake for 25 to 30 minutes until golden brown.

Remove to rack and cool slightly.

When cool, but slightly warm, apply the glaze.

BUTTERSCOTCH GEMS

These rolls require a 2-lb. piece of Danish dough (see page 119), gem sugar (see page 141), glaze (see page 142) and roll icing (see page 142).
Yield: 15 rolls

Grease a baking sheet.

On a well-floured surface, roll the 2-lb. piece of dough into a rectangle 15" tall and 18" wide.

Brush the top 1" edge with egg wash to seal and the remainder with 2 Tbs. of melted butter.

Visually divide the dough into three pieces from top to bottom.

Cover the center strip with gem sugar and fold the bottom flap up.

Wash the center of this newly formed strip with melted butter wash, cover with gem sugar and fold the top flap down to seal. The resulting piece is approximately 5" tall and 18" wide.

Lightly roll the piece with a small rolling pin to flatten. The piece should now be about 6" high and 24" wide.

With a knife, or better yet a pizza wheel cutter, cut the gems into 1½"-wide strips.

Twist the gems like a candy cane and place side by side on greased baking sheet.

Proof, covered, in a warm area until doubled in size.

Preheat oven to 375 degrees.

Place pan in the center of upper rack and bake for 25 to 30 minutes until golden brown.

While still a bit warm, glaze and drizzle from side to side with roll icing.

These were one of the top five most popular items at the bakery. Probably number three after schnecken and butter bits. I remember my mother-in-law Ruth and my daughter Carly packing pan after pan of the gooey gems in wax paper and stashing the ones that were ordered before the other customers could see them. They made such a game of this. It was so cute to watch them giggle and laugh, as if they were playing some secret spy game.

You can make the gems fifteen at a time, but again I recommend making more. Not because of the difficulty, but because you won't be able to keep these long. They have a habit of mysteriously disappearing. I remember pulling a full pan of six dozen gems out of the rack, only to find one plucked from the center. I wonder what happened? They are irresistible.

BUTTER DANISH ROLLS

These rolls require a 12-oz. piece of Danish dough (see page 119), buttercream filling (see page 138), yellow crumbs (see page 144), glaze (see page 142) and roll icing (see page 142).
Yield: 6 rolls

Grease a baking sheet or use a parchment-lined pan.

On a well-floured surface, roll the 12-oz. piece of dough into a rectangle 12" high and 6" wide.
Brush the bottom 1" edge with egg wash to seal.
Cover the dough with ½ cup of buttercream filling and sprinkle with ¼ cup of yellow crumbs.
Starting at the top, roll down the piece of dough and cut evenly into six rolls.
Place rolls, cut side up, on greased baking sheet.
Proof, covered, in a warm area until doubled in size.
Preheat oven to 375 degrees.
Place pan in the center of upper rack and bake for 25 to 30 minutes until golden brown.
While still a bit warm, glaze and ice with roll icing.

FILLED DANISH ROLLS

These rolls require a 12-oz. piece of Danish dough (see page 119), tea ring filling (see page 143), glaze (see page 142) and roll icing (see page 142).

Use the directions given for the butter Danish rolls with the following variations.
After the bottom 1" edge has been brushed with egg wash, wash the remainder of the dough with 2 Tbs. of melted butter. Cover the dough with 1 cup of tea ring filling before rolling the piece of dough.

FRUIT DANISH ROLLS

These rolls require a 12-oz. piece of Danish dough (see page 119), fruit filling (see page 141), cinnamon sugar (see page 140), cinnamon crumbs and yellow crumbs (see page 139 and 144), glaze (see page 142) and roll icing (see page 142).

Use the directions given for the butter Danish rolls with the following variations.

After the bottom 1" edge has been brushed with egg wash, wash the remainder of the dough with 2 Tbs. of melted butter, followed by 4 Tbs. of cinnamon sugar.

Starting at the top, roll down the piece of dough and cut evenly into six rolls. Place rolls, cut side up, on greased baking sheet and flatten them with your fingertips into 4" to 5" disks, forming a shallow cup with edges to hold the fruit. Do this by pressing from the center and forming a little edge around the outside. Fill the "cup" with fruit.

Top the apple filling with cinnamon crumbs (see page 139); top the other fruit fillings with yellow crumbs (see page 144).

While still a bit warm, glaze and drizzle from side to side with roll icing.

When cool water was needed for Danish recipes, Bill (as well as other bakers) developed the ability to know what temperature the water was by testing it with a finger. If it was above sixty-eight degrees, he'd throw in some ice to cool it down. Tap water could get too warm at certain times of the year.

What's even more amazing is that the same delicate, sensitive fingers that could determine slight differences in degrees of temperature could also handle hot stuff straight from the oven with bare hands.

CHEESE DANISH ROLLS

These rolls require a 12-oz. piece of Danish dough (see page 119), cheese filling (see page 149), glaze (see page 142) and cinnamon sugar (see page 140).

Follow the directions given above for the fruit Danish rolls, with the variation of substituting cheese filling for the fruit and eliminating the yellow crumb topping and roll icing. The cheese Danish are topped with a sprinkled dot of cinnamon.

Fillings, Frostings and Other Toppings

(in alphabetical order)

Buttercream Filling

2 cups sugar
¾ tsp. salt
5 oz. (½ cup + 2 Tbs.) shortening
4 oz. (1 stick) butter softened
2 eggs
4 Tbs. corn syrup
4 Tbs. all purpose flour
¼ cup milk
1 tsp. vanilla

This filling freezes well, and after thawing, the texture is identical to fresh. But the buttercream does separate fairly easily, so just make sure you stir the mixture after it has thawed to bring it back together before you put it on the cake.

Combine and cream first four ingredients.
Add eggs and corn syrup, scrape and mix well.
Add flour and mix.
Combine milk and vanilla.
Add, scrape bowl and mix until smooth.
Yield: three 10-oz. portions (approximately 3¾ cups)

CHOCOLATE GANACHE/ICING

> Replicating what Virginia Bakery used for a chocolate frosting is challenging because we used commercial items for the preparation, but here is a good chocolate ganache recipe that I use at home.

1 lb. dark or bittersweet chocolate (your choice; I like bittersweet)
12 oz. (1½ cups) heavy cream

Chunk the chocolate into small pieces in a stainless steel bowl.
Heat the cream to almost boiling (a microwave works great for this) and pour over the chocolate to cover. Let stand 10 minutes—no less.
Now mix until smooth, let cool and you have a delicious chocolate icing.
If you want a thicker icing, cut back on the cream. Thinner icing, use more cream. You can also add a little sugar to taste, but dissolve in hot cream first. You can also use milk chocolate but will need to cut the cream in half (6 ounces per pound of milk chocolate).
Yield: approximately 3 cups

CINNAMON CRUMBS

2 Tbs. butter
3 Tbs. shortening
⅓ cup sugar
⅓ cup light brown sugar loosely packed
1 tsp. honey optional, but desired
1 tsp. cinnamon
⅛ tsp. salt
Caramel color (optional)
⅔ cup all-purpose flour

Cream everything except flour.
Add the flour and rub between the tips of your fingers, kind of like mixing pie

> In the bakery, we would make the base, everything but the flour, and rub in the flour fresh every morning. Cinnamon crumbs will dry out quickly unless covered or refrigerated.
> The caramel color was added to darken the crumbs. Not necessary. If you do use it, don't use too much; it can be bitter. Caramel color is nothing but burnt sugar. Be careful if you make it at home—it smokes something awful.

dough. Do not combine flour in mixer; it is too easy to over mix. Mix until you have nice, moist cinnamon crumbs. If they are too wet, add more flour. If too dry, add a little melted butter.
Yield: 2 cups

CINNAMON SMEAR

1 cup light brown sugar
5 Tbs. butter
5 Tbs. shortening
2 tsp. cinnamon
¼ tsp. salt
Caramel color (optional)
3 Tbs. egg whites
4 Tbs. chocolate cake crumbs (you can use regular crumbs and add 1 tsp. cocoa powder)

Cream first six ingredients.
Add egg whites and mix.
Fold in cake crumbs.
Yield: approximately 1½ cups

CINNAMON SUGAR MIXTURE

1 cup of sugar with 1 tsp. of cinnamon

DOUGHNUT GLAZE

1½ cups powdered sugar
¼ cup water
1 Tbs. corn syrup
1 tsp. shortening
¼ tsp. vanilla

Heat all ingredients except powdered sugar and vanilla in saucepan until dissolved.

Remove from heat and add powdered sugar and then vanilla.

Thin with water if necessary.

Use while still warm.

Yield: 1 cup

FRUIT FILLING

> Vanilla can be a wonderful mellow addition to berries, while lemon juice will make them more tart, as some prefer.

Fresh berries (approximately 2 cups) need to be thickened with cornstarch or tapioca before baking. If using cherries, the pits need to be removed before measuring.

To each cup of berries, add a mixture of 1 tsp. cornstarch or tapioca, ¼ cup sugar and a pinch of salt. If you like, you can also add a few drops of vanilla or lemon juice—not both.

For apple filling, peel, core, slice and dice, if desired, about 3 apples. Combine ¼ cup sugar, 1 tsp. flour, ½ tsp. cinnamon and a pinch of salt. Mix the dry ingredients with the apples. As with the berries, vanilla or lemon juice can be added if desired.

FRUIT-FLAVORED ICING

Follow directions for making white buttercream icing and add fruit flavoring. At the bakery, we used products called fruit ice, which were the consistency of a very thick jam and were made with whole fruit. At home, you can use jam. Starting with 1 Tbs. of jam, add until you get the desired effect and flavor.

GEM SUGAR

1 cup brown sugar
½ pecan pieces
2 Tbs. melted butter

Combine all.

Glaze

Combine equal parts of corn syrup and water and heat to blend.
When indicated, brush this mixture over the top of rolls and coffee cakes while still warm from the oven.

Roll Icing

¼ cup water
¼ cup light corn syrup
¼ cup granulated sugar
1 Tbs. shortening
½ tsp. salt
3 cups powdered sugar
1 tsp. vanilla
½ tsp. egg white (optional)

Put the ¼ cup water in your measuring cup. Add the ¼ cup corn syrup to bring your total to ½ cup.
Place these in a small saucepan.
Add the granulated sugar, shortening and salt. Bring to a boil and dissolve the sugar.
Off heat, add the powdered sugar, the vanilla and egg white.
The icing will at first appear very thin; it will thicken upon cooling. Like all recipes, feel free to adjust it.
Yield: 2 cups

Schnecken Goo

1 cup brown sugar
4 Tbs. shortening
3 Tbs. butter
⅛ tsp. salt
1 Tbs. corn syrup
½ Tbs. honey
½ Tbs. water

Cream all the ingredients in a bowl.
Yield: approximately 1½ cups

TEA RING FILLING

1¼ cups sugar
½ tsp. salt
¼ cup + 1 Tbs. almond paste
1 Tbs. cinnamon
10 oz. pecan pieces
¾ cup water
¼ cup honey
¾ cup shortening
4 Tbs. butter
6 cups bread crumbs—see note

Combine sugar, salt and almond paste in mixer until well blended.
Add cinnamon and combine.
Put mixture in large mixing bowl and add pecans.
Combine water, honey, shortening and butter in a saucepan and heat until fats dissolve.
Add to mixing bowl.
Add crumbs and mix well.
Yield: 10 cups
This filling freezes well.

Bread crumbs—In a real bakery you would have stales, or leftovers, that would be ground up for crumbs and used in different fillings such as this or cinnamon smear. We would use a lot of different items for crumbs, such as doughnuts, breads and rolls.

At home you can do the same thing. Save leftover bakery items or bread, dry them and grind them in a Cuisinart or blender. You can even put them in a strong plastic bag and mash them with a rolling pin. Do not use items with raisins, seeds or weird flavorings you wouldn't want in your filling.

WHITE BUTTERCREAM ICING

4 cups powdered sugar
10 Tbs. shortening
2 Tbs. butter
¼ tsp. salt
4 Tbs. Angel White Fudge Ice (optional)
1 tsp. vanilla
1 egg white

Mix sugar, shortening, butter and salt (and Angel White if using it) until it starts to come together.
Add vanilla and mix.

In order to make this the same as at the bakery, you will need to track down some Angel White Fudge Ice icing base, a commercial preparation similar to fondant. It helped to stabilize and firm the icing.

I'm providing the original recipe and, if you can find the angel white base, great. If not, don't worry. I've made the icing at home without the base, and it works just fine. I just wanted you to know there will be a difference.

Add egg white and cream on low speed, scraping bowl once or twice until icing is smooth.

Yield: This makes a little more than one store-bought can of icing and should be enough to ice one 8" cake.

YELLOW CRUMBS

1 cup sugar
¼ tsp. salt
4 oz. shortening
2 oz. butter
1 Tbs. corn syrup
1 egg yolk
1½ tsp. vanilla
Flour (approximately ⅔ cup)
A few drops yellow food color

I'm not a big fan of artificial color, but I use it for yellow crumbs. You don't have to.

Cream sugar, salt, shortening and butter.

Add remaining ingredients, scrape bowl and mix well.

When ready to make crumbs, add and rub in enough (preferably) winter flour to make a soft moist crumb.

Yield: 2 cups

Front Shop Recipes

The recipes in this chapter are all uniquely individual, as they are not made from master doughs, such as the coffee cakes and many breads are made, and they cover a variety of sweet baked goods from fancy to plain.

The chocolate éclairs and cream puffs were among many customers' favorite items. Writing about Howard Thie, Deborah Rieselman wrote in her *Clifton Living* article that

> *fresh cream is the secret to his popular éclairs and cream puffs. Bakers generally use a mix to make their éclair filling, says Cindy, Howard's wife. "But no matter how good the mix, it never tastes as good as homemade," she says.*
>
> *She should know. One summer she and Howard tried a mix. It was the only way to make éclairs year round…their homemade custard spoils too easily in summer if customers let the éclairs sit around in the heat.*
>
> *The summer that the Thies tried a mix, éclair sales slowly dropped for several months. When the mix was discontinued in the fall, sales were equally slow to return to normal because customers were unaware of what was going on. The Thies have never brought a mix through their door again. "You just have to use quality ingredients to get quality products," Mrs. Thie simply states. "If you have a good business, you must be doing something right, so we've learned there's no reason to change it."*

Amy Nadicksbernd's family was among the fans.

> *I have very fond memories of my grandfather coming over to our house and bringing us the enormous yummy éclairs, and that was a very special treat. In fact, when I became old enough to drive, my mother would send me to… get the éclairs, when* [my grandfather] *could no longer drive. As an adult, I stopped by the bakery to pick up the éclairs and the bakery was no longer in business. I was heartbroken. The bakery provided fond memories for me and my family. Everything was delicious; we just loved the éclairs the best. I have lived in several states and have never found anything comparable. They were so large, with wonderful pudding and heavenly chocolate icing. Such a treat!*

This sentiment was corroborated by others. The Templeton family recalled that the reason the chocolate éclairs were so good was because "they had the really good pudding in them—not the cheap whipped cream stuff that others have in them. They were the best because of the filling and the chocolate was thick and not runny—so good. And the éclair shells did not get mushy." Sandy Schneeman spoke of her grandmother, Cora Samad, who worked at the bakery, stating that the things she really enjoyed at Virginia Bakery were her fellow workers, the owner Mr. Thie and the éclairs.

Cream puffs were similar to the éclairs—they just didn't have the chocolate topping. Having one of these items served for dessert was a special treat.

CREAM PUFFS

¼ cup milk
¾ cup water
3 Tbs. shortening
1 Tbs. butter
⅔ cup bread flour
¼ tsp. salt
⅛ tsp. baking powder
½ cup eggs

Bring milk, water and fats to boil in a heavy saucepan or the metal bowl of your mixer.
Combine flour, salt and baking powder.

Add to the mixture in the pan and cook at least one minute, stirring with a wooden spoon.

You are trying to cook out the moisture. The mix, known as *pâte à choux*, should form a tight ball and become shiny.

Remove from heat and let stand about 3 minutes.

Gradually whip in eggs in four increments, making sure each egg is well incorporated before adding another.

Transfer the warm mixture to a piping bag with a 1" piping tip. Pipe *pâte à choux* on parchment-lined baking sheets, creating 2½" balls. Leave space between them; they need room for expansion.

Preheat oven to 425 degrees.

Place baking sheet in the oven.

After ten minutes, reduce heat to 350 degrees and bake about 20 more minutes until the puffs are golden brown.

Remove from oven and let cool before filling.

Yield: 1 dozen puff shells

To fill the puff, put custard in pastry bag with ¼" piping tip.

Poke hole in shell with a clean wooden dowel or a small knife.

Pipe the custard in through this hole.

Cream puffs are dusted with powdered sugar.

THE WORLD'S BEST CUSTARD

3 Tbs. cornstarch
2 cups milk
¾ cup sugar
⅛ tsp. salt
3 egg yolks
1 tsp. vanilla

Dissolve cornstarch in ¼ cup milk, making a slurry.

Combine remaining milk, sugar, salt and egg yolks in a heavy saucepan.

Bring to a boil, stirring occasionally.

Add cornstarch slurry and cook, stirring until thickened.

Remove from heat, stirring occasionally.

Fold in vanilla when cooler.

Allow custard to cool completely before filling shells…and keep your fingers out of it. It'll be hard to do.

CHOCOLATE ÉCLAIRS

I don't know why, but I really like making these. I'm not sure whether it is the skill level involved or the way I remember my dad standing over the back stove making the "World's Best Custard" that would fill my favorite pastry. Actually, as I recall cracking open the cream puffs, sucking out the custard and throwing the shell away, I think it was the custard that was the best part. For a real treat, Dad would make some extra custard and bring it home in little plastic tubs for dessert on Saturday night. He was thoughtful like that.

The *pâte à choux* (pronounced paht ah shoo) is a cooked dough. *Choux* actually means cabbage in French, which is what a cream puff resembles. You can do this by hand, but a stand mixer makes it a lot easier.

We would make two weeks' worth of éclair and cream puff shells ahead of time and keep the empty shells in the freezer. When we wanted to make them, we'd pull out two or three dozen at a time, make the filling, add the filling to the shells and put them out for sale.

Follow the directions for making cream puffs with the following changes.

When piping the *pâte à choux* on parchment-lined baking sheets, make 5" tubes for the éclairs.

Yield: 1 dozen éclairs

To fill the éclair, put custard in pastry bag with ¼" piping tip.

Poke hole in one end of shell with a clean wooden dowel or a small knife.

Pipe the custard in through this hole.

Éclairs are topped with a coating of chocolate ganache (see page 139).

Howard cutting cheesecake in the front shop.

Unlike some of the light and airy styles of cheesecake available in grocery stores, Virginia Bakery's German cheesecakes had substance. While some customers loved the flavor of the yeast dough combined with the cheese filling, others preferred the graham cracker crust. Some were convinced that cheesecake was a healthy choice. After all, there was the protein from the cheese and eggs and a sort of bread-like crust, making it the best "sandwich" possible.

Marilyn Bixler stated that after schnecken, Virginia Bakery cheesecakes were her "second favorite thing in the whole world." Judy Ganace, as a child, considered the cheesecake to be a rather adult item. "I still see that cheesecake as golden and simple. It was definitely more cake-like than the New York style you mostly see today."

CHEESECAKE

Filling:
¾ cup sugar
⅛ tsp. salt
2 Tbs. flour
3 Tbs. cornstarch
3 Tbs. shortening
2 eggs

> Whether you use a graham cracker crust or a sweet dough crust, the filling is the same.
> Our cheesecake is not a sweet New York type cheesecake, but rather a slightly sour German version.

1 lb. Farmer's Cheese (If you are unable to find Farmer's Cheese, cottage cheese that has been drained for an hour, using cheesecloth or a coffee filter, will work)
½ tsp. lemon juice
¼ cup buttermilk
½ cup milk

Combine first four ingredients and cream in the shortening, then the eggs. Place everything in a blender and blend smooth.

This is best made in advance so the mixture can rest in the refrigerator at least an hour before using. I used to make it the night before and let it set up.

Yield: enough filling for 1 cake

Make the crust of your choice.
Preheat oven to 350 degrees.
Fill the crust with cheese mixture.
You can lightly sprinkle cinnamon over cheese before baking if you like.
Place pan in the center of upper rack and bake in a low oven for about 1 hour until the cheese filling has set.

Crusts
To make the graham crust, grind 16 graham cracker squares in a Cuisinart.
Add approximately 4 Tbs. of melted butter to moisten them.
Press firmly into the bottom of your pan. An 8" x 8" glass baking dish works well for this.

For the sweet dough crust, grease an 8" round cake pan.
Use a 7-oz. piece of yellow dough and press into the pan, forming a lip around the sides to contain the cheese.

The moist and dense brownies with the wonderful chocolate frosting were among the items customers always bought. A few people were lucky enough to get them for free. Cherie Lynn Sauer shared the story about how her grandfather, Gus Nolte, would send home leftover pastries on Monday from Saturday's baked goods. "When my daddy brought a bag home, we were always excited to see what was inside. Not until many years later did I realize that brownies came in squares, because we got the strips cut from the sides of brownies!"

BROWNIES

¾ cup sugar
⅛ tsp. salt
4 Tbs. corn syrup
2 Tbs. shortening
2 Tbs. butter
2 Tbs. pre-melted chocolate
    liquor or 1 oz. melted
    bittersweet chocolate pieces
1 egg
2 Tbs. water
½ cup cake flour
½ cup pecan pieces

Cream the first six ingredients.
Add egg and water, scrape bowl and whip until creamy using paddle attachment of a mixer.
Fold in flour and pecans.
Pour batter into a greased 8" x 8" cake pan. Not necessary, but for those who want to be able to lift the brownies out of the pan easily, place parchment paper in the greased pan with two sides overhanging the pan edge.
Preheat oven to 350 degrees.
Place pan in the center of upper rack and bake for approximately 35 to 40 minutes.
Brownies will appear soft, but they will set when cool. Do not over-bake.
After brownies have cooled, frost while in the pan with chocolate ganache (see page 139) or a buttercream icing of your choice and cut into squares.

Bran muffins were one of Virginia Bakery's well-known specialties. Some folks referred to them as "wheat gems." Many people confirmed the idea that Virginia Bakery made the best bran muffins in the city, whether they preferred the plain ones or the ones with raisins. Susan Newmark, a devotee of the muffins, made the comment that "other places typically make bran muffins that are dry and tasteless. The ones at Virginia Bakery were incredibly moist and slightly sweeter—they had a lot of flavor—a real treat. They were more exciting to eat than regular bran muffins. The sticky glaze made them slightly sweeter, but you could still feel as if you were eating something healthy."

Judy Ganance echoed that love:

> Bran muffins!! They were the favorite from Virginia Bakery. They were probably only about thirty cents when we started our routine of buying them. My mom…didn't allow us to buy cookies very often, so bran muffins were clearly the healthy choice. I know I would still love them today. They were crumbly, light muffins that were baked and turned over on a wire rack; they were coated with a honey and brown sugar glaze. The texture ranged from gooey with glaze on top to crispy on the bottom edges. If Mom wouldn't notice I would sneak into the bag and tear off an edge and eat it secretly. Later, as teenagers, we would take them camping, and while they might get smushed in our backpacks, we'd scavenge every crumb.

In my own family's case, my father and I shared a fondness for bran muffins. When the count got down to the last one in the box or bag, I felt as if I had to leave it until I checked that he didn't want it and I could have the last one. They were definitely tasty by themselves, but putting grape jam on them was an added flavor treat.

Bran muffins were made on a daily basis. Similar to schnecken, once the muffin molds came out of the ovens, the items were flipped out onto a sheet pan.

BRAN MUFFINS

1½ cups schnecken goo (see page 142)
2 Tbs. butter
6 Tbs. shortening
2 cups fine wheat flour
2 cups wheat bran
1 Tbs. baking powder
⅔ cup sugar
⅛ tsp. salt
2 eggs
2 cups milk
1 cup raisins (optional) per dozen

Yield: 2 dozen muffins

Prepare the pans by greasing 2 dozen muffin molds and spreading 1 Tbs. of schnecken goo in the bottom of each cup. Melt the butter and shortening. Combine the flour, bran and baking powder.
In your mixing bowl, combine the sugar, salt and eggs.
Add the milk and blend well.
Add the flour mix and then mix in the melted fats.
Add raisins if you like. Alternatively, fill 1 dozen molds for plain and then add raisins to the batter and make a dozen with raisins.
Divide the batter equally between the molds, filling each cup about ⅔ full.
Preheat oven to 375 degrees.
Place pans in the center of upper rack and bake for about 20 minutes, until centers are set.
Turn out onto a baking sheet.

Cakes

A 1960 *Vitality News* article that featured an interview with Bill Thie, who was labeled "successful merchandiser," noted that cakes were big sellers for Virginia Bakery, and "Bill [summed] up his thoughts on wedding, birthday and specialty cakes by saying 'they are a must for retail bakers.'" Whether customers came in for regular dessert varieties, birthday cakes, holiday specialties or wedding cakes, Virginia Bakery had a large assortment of wonderful frosted items to choose from. To this day, many former customers still compare in their minds the cakes they are eating with the memories of the cakes they bought at Virginia Bakery and how much they loved them.

Among the most popular dessert cakes was Bill's simple single-layer cake. However, some occasions merited one of the fancier and more intricate cakes, like a Dobash torte with many layers interspersed by bittersweet chocolate, a German chocolate cake with sugary coconut and chopped nut filling or an angel food cake covered in icing. Holidays, such as Easter, had customers coming in wanting themed cakes like bunny cakes or the traditionally favorite lamb cakes for the spring celebration.

For regular customers, buying their families' birthday cakes from Virginia Bakery was a given, except for those unfortunate enough to have their birthdays fall during the two weeks each summer that the bakery closed for vacation. Helen Adams shared, "My favorite treat was always the chocolate cake with white icing. Every year on my birthday the bakery was closed for vacation! Every year I anticipated the inevitable disappointment I would feel on my birthday."

But for those lucky enough to be born during the other fifty weeks of each year, some of their best memories were of their birthday cakes. For many children, there was great excitement in going to the bakery and looking over all the little novelty items, and there was often some difficulty in deciding which of the cake decorations on display and which flavor of cake would be chosen for that year's celebration. Zachary Green's favorite memory as a young boy was not the wonderful smells and tastes, but rather the visuals. He always thought of a trip to Virginia Bakery as being similar to a trip to a very interesting children's museum because of all the birthday cake displays.

> *They circled above the counters with mirrors reflecting their images to the customers. Every time we would visit, I would spend the entire time looking up at the dozens of amazing sculptures in icing of Batman, Superman, Incredible Hulk, clowns and Sesame Street characters, to name a few. I always had the hardest time a few weeks before my birthday because I could not choose which cake I wanted to select! Now that I have my own five-year-old, I drive by Ludlow with a lump in my throat because my son will have to choose his next birthday cake from an online catalogue rather than the wonderful mirrored display of Virginia Bakery cake clowns.*

Birthday celebrations were the reason for some very unique cakes as well. Jane Knueven remembered how she was ecstatic the year her brother, Ed Arnult (a Virginia Bakery employee), brought home "the biggest, most beautiful cake I ever had! Boy was I surprised when we tried to cut it…it was one of the bakery's display cakes; so it was cardboard covered with icing!… icing on cardboard!" She was a bit disappointed with his joke, but she ate most of the icing anyway.

Howard Sahnd, the director of a funeral home across the street from Virginia Bakery, became friends with the bakers and made weekly, if not daily, visits at the bakery's back door. One time, his wife had a dinner party for his birthday and the bakers decided to play a trick on Howard. They made a black cake with black icing and wrote, "Happy Birthday Digger O'Dell" on top because he was the "undertaker." (Digger O'Dell was the name of a character, the friendly undertaker, on the popular 1940s radio show *The Life of Riley*.) Mrs. Sahnd was not at all happy when she opened up the box and was appalled by the joke, but other family members found the incident humorous and indicative of the bakers' sense of humor.

Laurie Bredenfoerder shared a story about another novel cake she ordered for her mother, "a lightly closeted bakery icing fanatic who can hardly control herself around a birthday cake." One year, anticipating her mother's upcoming celebration, she had "one of the most fabulous ideas of [her] life…and Virginia Bakery's bakers were co-conspirators." The cake was to be "all icing—no cake at all." The clerk was so uncomfortable committing to the order that she called a baker to the counter to make sure it could be done. After asking numerous questions to make sure everyone understood what she was wanting, the baker and cake decorator agreed to interrupt their normal routine long enough to help Laurie's vision come true.

> *The white bakery-icing "cake" was about the size of a butter plate and about three inches high on the side. It was beautifully decorated with pink roses and green garlands—and in the center, they'd written "Happy Birthday" in yellow icing…That marvelous one-of-a-kind piece of art…That "cake" represents the kind of personal service, flexibility and customer-centered spirit that, just as surely as the schnecken, has woven the Virginia Bakery into the collected lore that defines this city.*

While the more unusual cakes described above may have needed extra time to execute, customers had the option to pick out a cake and wait for it to be decorated if that suited their schedule better. As the "Cincinnati Bakery Tour" article reported, a decorator was on hand until 6:00 p.m. Birthday cake orders also provided an additional marketing tool for the Thies: records of the orders, from more than five thousand customers at the time the 1960 *Vitality News* feature article was written, provided a valuable mailing list for reaching customers with advertising material.

Although no specifics for making or decorating a wedding cake are provided in this book, there are some fascinating stories about this subject worthy of sharing. The same moist, delicious, from scratch Virginia Bakery cake batter that was used by the bakery in 1927 through the year 2005 was the basis of not only the dessert cakes but also the wedding cakes. In the earlier years, most of the wedding cakes were usually glorified birthday cakes. As the years went on, the process of decorating wedding cakes became an art unto itself, especially in the hands of both Cindy and Moe Thie. As contributor and relative, Marilyn Leathers wrote,

Seriously, this was Cindy's first cake. She had more talent and desire than anyone I knew.

Neither Cindy nor Maureen started their careers to become artists, but their beautifully decorated wedding/birthday/party cakes were legendary. Such imagination and artistic skill! The meticulous handwork that was involved! Maureen took additional training and always styled up with the latest (sometimes quirky) trends. It seemed that she and Cindy poured their hearts and souls into this talent. We all benefited! Now, years after the bakery has gone, Cincinnati is still raving about their beautiful cakes! What a nice legacy…

And a very true statement. Countless people, even those who were not Clifton regulars, shared that there was no question when they married that they had wanted to have Virginia Bakery make their wedding cake because of the bakery's reputation and the fact that they wanted the best for their significant day.

According to the February 1989 *Bakery* article:

Cindy Thie is known for the delicate precision of her decorating style. Although she has been decorating for only 10 years, she has developed a distinctive look that relies on satin-smooth icing, precision drapery and fine touches of color and detail. Her careful attention to icing preparation forms the foundation for picture-perfect cakes.

To achieve a glass-smooth finish, Cindy uses a food processor to blend her icings before applying them to cakes. Processing the mixed icings eliminates any tiny lumps or large air holes that could produce a rough surface. She ices her cakes while they are chilled, and takes special care to evenly coat wedding tiers. Before completing the process, she refrigerates the iced cakes, then uses a knife dipped in hot water to remove excess icing at the edges and to completely smooth the surface.

Icing processed in a food processor also works well for string work. Because processing the icing tends to heat it slightly, Cindy refrigerates the processed icing for using it to apply strings. Because all the large air bubbles have been eliminated, her string-work seldom breaks, allowing her to overlap strings and weave designs that never have to be repaired.

Because so many brides request strong or unusual colors on their cakes, such as black and royal blue, Cindy compromises by using those colors only as an accent. She may add one set of royal blue strings, dot on tiny royal blue drop flowers, or stripe her ribbon bag lightly. The overall effect is quite pleasing, satisfying the customer's color preference while creating a visually attractive cake.

Mary Ann Acree, as an active member of the Greater Cincinnati Retail Bakers Association, saw Cindy giving seminars and presentations at local and national events where she taught how to make wedding cakes. "She created nuptial confections that were known for miles around and frequently calmed nervous brides with the advice, 'Just don't worry about it; it will be beautiful.' Cindy was a true artist when it came to wedding cakes, sometimes spending fourteen hours on them when someone else might take three or four."

When Cindy was diagnosed with cancer in 1990, she began teaching Moe how to decorate wedding cakes. A couple of days before New Year's Eve 1992, while they were in this transition phase, Cindy's white count dropped very low, and Tom had to take his mother to the hospital. As they left, Cindy told Moe she was going to have to finish decorating the cake for an upcoming wedding. Moe was a nervous wreck and "probably smoked a pack of cigarettes trying to start decorating the cake," but she talked to herself and did the job. When Cindy got back home, she went to the refrigerator to look at the cake. "Absolutely not. Young lady, you are not going anywhere. We are redoing this whole cake." Moe first cried, then got mad, and that was the turning point. Moe worked all night. The next morning, Cindy came down from the upstairs apartment, and Moe told her

Cindy, being self-taught, developed her own methods of working with icing and gladly shared them. Almost every decorator is using a food processor now.

that she was ready for her to see the finished cake. With a tear in her eye, Cindy said, "Girl, you've got it now." Moe then felt that she could handle the situation—she was going to do this for Cindy. Moe learned a couple of things that night: a cake, unless it drops and falls apart, can be re-iced many times; and she needed to do her own design, not try to do what she thought Cindy would have done.

After Cindy's death, when Moe started handling the wedding cakes on her own, she admits that she didn't really know what she was doing. She didn't feel confident about how to decorate, so she worried about how she was going to sell her first cake. A father, mother and daughter came into the bakery. At the time, a piece of plaster was hanging from the ceiling and looked as if it was about to fall down. There was Moe struggling, practically doing handstands to sell the cake, but she didn't really know how to answer all the questions because she hadn't done this on her own before. The father looked up at the ceiling, looked at Moe and said to his daughter, "You know, she really doesn't know what she's doing, but I feel sorry for them because they really need a new ceiling and she needs a start. Pick her and give her some confidence." Luckily, they loved the cake and spread the good word.

Over the years, Moe became very skilled at decorating and learned to run the wedding cake department, handling everything from the first call, meeting with the bride and helping with the selections through delivery and setting up the cake for the reception. Virginia Bakery also had contracts with the (Hilton) Omni Netherland hotel, the Cincinnati Club and the Banker's Club to make their wedding cakes. Annie Glenn observed Moe's "desire to provide superior service to all customers. She was so talented artistically. And she treated everyone with compassion. I knew I was working for one of the most talented cake decorators in the world. She wanted to make 'her' brides' weddings perfect. And that usually meant with a cake. But she went the extra mile on so many levels."

The beautiful cakes, which were always artistically designed and carefully crafted by the Virginia Bakery decorators, came in all different sizes, styles, colors and shapes. Some brides supplied photos to be replicated. Others requested fresh floral arrangements to grace the top of the cake. The majority of brides over the years requested yellow or white cakes with white icing and maybe roses and sprinkled silver accents, but often enough people would ask for other choices, like chocolate cake or carrot or banana cake with cream cheese frosting. In several cases, the cakes were filled with fresh raspberries grown on the Thies' own bushes.

No matter what the design, delivering a wedding cake without damage was a tricky thing. Before the wedding cake was even put into the delivery van, those assigned the task needed to ask questions about where they should enter the building and which way the doors swung open. Cindy taught Jerry Armstead how to assemble the wedding cakes and how to fit them in the vehicle so they wouldn't slide. "There were some accidents, but she taught me how to repair them. She sent me with icing and everything I might need." Once in a while, an accident would cause him to have to take the cake back. "They were top heavy…things were going to happen…Tom's father, Howard, made the cakes special order; it's not like there were extras." Jerry would assemble them after he got to where the reception was being held: "the three-tiered type, the ones that had fountains and stairs coming down…all styles." Cindy made Jerry's wedding cake and a groom's cake, and he added, "I didn't have to deliver it either!"

The bakers at Virginia Bakery made cakes every day except Saturday, which was delivery day for wedding cakes. The method they used won't be found in any cookbooks and is not a classical method, but it obviously worked because the comment the Thie family always got was "Not only was it beautiful, but it tasted good, as well"—as if the customers expected the cakes not to. Tom says the method is very easy. "It's almost as quick as a box mix and ten times better."

General Cake Information

How to treat cakes: This is what I learned over the many years of baking cakes.

Most books say to use greased and floured pans, which works, but I find it easier to remove the cakes if you line the bottom with parchment as well. At the bakery, we lined the sides of the pan as well. This helps keep a crust from forming, which made it easier to trim the cakes for icing. If you want, you can do this at home as well. Just cut strips of paper a little higher than your pan and press against the sides.

Frozen cakes are moister and taste better than fresh cakes. I don't know why, but they do. I've gone to several sources, including Alton Brown of *Good Eats* fame and even the CIA, my alma mater. No answers. My theory is there is a redistribution of the moisture when a cake is frozen and then thawed. You won't find this tip in any other baking books, at least none I've seen so far.

At the bakery, after baking and removing the cakes from the pan, they were allowed to cool. They were then saran wrapped and frozen overnight. Not only did this make the cake taste better, but it also made it much easier for the decorator to ice. A fresh cake is much harder to ice than one that has been frozen. Now here's the kicker. Almost every wedding cake we sold was frozen and then thawed. I'm sorry to all those brides who demanded fresh cake, but believe me, this method worked better. Every complaint we had about stale cake, of which I can only remember three, was the result of having to ice a fresh cake. After the cake was iced and smoothed, it was placed back in the freezer until it was ready to be decorated.

This is the IMPORTANT part. Never pull a cake directly from the freezer and thaw it at room temperature. It will "sweat," and you will have a terrible mess. Put the cake in the refrigerator for several hours, allowing it to slowly come up to temperature. I think this is where the redistribution of moisture takes place. You can now remove it from the fridge and decorate it or allow it to come to room temperature and serve. If you want to experiment, try it both ways. Let me know what happens.

THE THREE BASIC CAKE RECIPES

YELLOW WINDSOR CAKE

⅞ cup sugar
2 tsp. baking powder
½ tsp. salt
1⅓ cups cake flour
7 Tbs. vegetable shortening
½ cup + 1 Tbs. milk
2 eggs
½ tsp. vanilla

Combine sugar, baking powder and salt. Put aside.
Cream flour and shortening in mixing bowl about 5 minutes. No need to sift flour.
Stop mixer, add 1 Tbs. milk and scrape bowl.
Add sugar mixture and cream about 5 minutes.
Combine remaining ½ cup milk, eggs and vanilla. Add to batter, ⅓ at a time, scraping bowl well after each addition. Mix 2 minutes on medium speed between each addition and after the last addition. See how easy that is.
Divide your batter into two 8" square greased and parchment-lined cake pans.
Preheat oven to 375 degrees.
Place pans in the center of upper rack and bake for 25 to 30 minutes.
Test for doneness by pressing on the center of the cake. If it is firm and springs back, it is done.

Yield: two 8" square cakes or two dozen cupcakes

WHITE CAKE

For white cake, just substitute 4 ounces (¹/₂ cup) of egg whites for the 2 eggs that are in the yellow cake recipe.

⅞ cup sugar
2 tsp. baking powder
¹/₂ tsp. salt
1⅓ cups cake flour
7 Tbs. vegetable shortening
¹/₂ cup + 1 Tbs. milk
4 oz. of egg whites
¹/₂ tsp. vanilla

I know some people will consider this as cheating, but this is what happened at the bakery, and everyone seemed to like it. Voila, the white cake.

CHOCOLATE CAKE

1 cup sugar
1 tsp. baking soda
⅛ tsp. baking powder
¹/₂ tsp. salt
4 Tbs. cocoa powder

1⅓ cups cake flour
6 Tbs. vegetable shortening
⅞ cup buttermilk (you can use whole milk with 1 tsp. white vinegar added)
2 eggs
½ tsp. vanilla

Combine sugar, baking soda, baking powder, salt and cocoa. Put aside.
Cream flour and shortening in mixing bowl about 5 minutes. No need to sift flour.
Stop mixer, add 1 Tbs. buttermilk and scrape bowl.
Add sugar mixture and cream about 5 minutes.
Combine remaining buttermilk, eggs and vanilla. Add to batter, ⅓ at a time, scraping bowl well after each addition. Mix 2 minutes on medium speed between each addition and after the last addition. See how easy that is.
Divide your batter into two 8" square greased and parchment-lined cake pans.
Preheat oven to 375 degrees.
Place pans in the center of upper rack and bake for 25 to 30 minutes.
Test for doneness by pressing on the center of the cake. If it is firm and springs back, it is done.

Yield: two 8" square cakes or two dozen cupcakes

DOBASH TORTE

> This was many customers' favorite cake. My cousin Paul loved this cake, and so do I. The chocolate filling is what makes the cake.

Follow the directions for making the Windsor yellow cake (see page 162), but divide the batter into three 8" round pans.

After the cakes are baked and cooled, each layer will be sliced in half, giving you six layers to be filled.

At the bakery we used round cake pans, but at home I prefer to use square cake pans, as the cakes are easier to slice when serving. The choice is yours.

DOBASH FILLING

2 cups water
3 Tbs. cornstarch
1 ¼ cups sugar
4 Tbs. shortening
¼ tsp. salt
2 Tbs. corn syrup
6 Tbs. cocoa powder

Reserve ¼ cup of the water and dissolve the cornstarch in it to make a slurry. Put the rest of the ingredients in a medium saucepan along with the sugar, salt and corn syrup. Bring to a boil.
Whisk in cocoa powder.
Add cornstarch slurry and whisk constantly until mixture thickens.
Remove from heat and cool.

Yield: This makes enough to fill and decorate one Dobash torte

To assemble the torte, start with a layer of cake. Then alternate layers of filling and cake, topping with a final layer of cake.
Save a little of the filling to decorate the top of the torte after it is iced.

The whole cake gets iced with buttercream icing (see page 143).
The sides get toasted coconut pressed into them, and the top is decorated with a little Dobash filling.

ANGEL FOOD CAKE

2 cups egg whites room temp.
1 cup sugar
½ tsp. vanilla
⅛ tsp. salt
1 tsp. cream of tartar
1¼ cups sugar
1¼ cups cake flour

Whip egg whites and vanilla until soft peaks form.

Mix salt and cream of tartar with 1 cup of sugar and gradually whip in until stiff peaks form.

Combine remaining sugar and cake flour.

Remove bowl from mixer and with a clean rubber spatula gently fold this mixture in, adding one half at a time.

Place batter in a clean angel food cake mold or Bundt pan— a 9" tube pan, about 6" deep.

Preheat oven to 350 degrees.

Place pan in the center of upper rack and bake approximately 40 minutes until top is golden brown. Remove from oven and turn pan upside down on a plate or parchment-lined baking pan. Allow to cool this way a least one hour before removing from pan.

Yield: 1 cake

The most difficult part about making angel food cake is working grease free. I would wash my mixing bowl, whip and molds in hot water with a cup of vinegar to cut any residual grease. Any fat will hinder the proper formation of the egg whites upon whipping. If your cake falls or doesn't rise, it is probably due to some fat along the way.

The easiest way to remove it is to bang the rim of the mold on a cutting board until the cake releases.

Many people enjoyed these plain; others loved icing coating the top and dripping down the sides. Most times the icing used was the buttercream (see page 143), but others asked for chocolate (see page 139) or cherry (see page 142).

166

Pies

Virginia Bakery did a wonderful pie business from the time Bill opened the bakery doors in 1927. Some people reported buying one daily. During any given week, the bakers made a large variety of pies. The standard fruit pies were made every day, such as apple, cherry and blueberry, but each day of the week also had a specialty pie, such as custard, pecan, lemon meringue, coconut custard or Dutch apple. During the fall and winter holidays, pumpkin and mince joined the ranks. There were some seasonal restrictions. The banana, coconut, chocolate, butterscotch and other cream pies were only made in the cooler weather. Karen Striet remembers how she got her friend Jackie a job at the bakery during their first year in college. Her friend's first day occurred during the one month out of the year that they baked strawberry whipped cream pies. These particular pies were only baked as special orders (very seldom doubled or made for the cases). People in the know had placed their orders in advance. Jackie was carrying a tray with six pies and slipped. "They all went flying—all special orders, and more couldn't be made!" Karen shared that Jackie still talks about that day and has nightmares about the event.

According to Bill Thie's daughter, Sandy, the work of running the bakery was a labor of love, and her father enjoyed pleasing the customers. One time she remembers vividly was when two of her friends stopped in the bakery and she introduced them to her father. Just to get a reaction, Bill cut an eight-inch strawberry whipped cream pie in half and handed a

Gus Nolte, Carl Thie and other pie makers. I can only guess how many pies were made on that table. *Courtesy of the Gus Nolte family.*

full half pie to each of them. He provided no plate, no forks—just a piece of wax paper under each half—and said, "Taste this and tell me what you think." "Eyes got really wide. I was shocked and still cannot remember what my friends did."

Sandy also recalled how the pie orders were taken and provided a description of the lists that were used in the back of the bakery. The ladies in the order department would write the pie names on big sheets of paper, along with who ordered them, so that the bakers knew how many to make and who to box them up for. The ladies would draw a line, tally up the number and hang the tally sheet over near Carl so he knew how many, plus a few, to make.

Over time, the pie and cake lists dwindled in direct proportion to the availability of frozen pies and cakes in the grocery stores. More women were working outside their homes, and they liked one-stop shopping at the grocery. "While for some taste did not matter," Sandy said, "we did still have our die-hard customers who knew quality goods." For them, making the extra stop was well worth the effort.

As I write this, I can't help but think about how many pies slid over the front bench in seventy-five years. I love the old photo with the bench covered in pies and my Uncle Carl beaming proudly. Pie making was a real talent, and we took a lot of pride in it. I wonder how many Thanksgiving dinners we "attended" through this God-given talent. Makes you think, doesn't it?

Holidays, especially Thanksgiving, were tough. I remember getting up at one o'clock in the morning to start the pies for Thanksgiving and Christmas. Pies were one thing that could not be baked ahead of time; they had to be fresh. Fortunately, pie making is a lot like cooking Asian food. There's a lot of time-consuming prep work, but the final product comes together quickly. And par-baked shells could be made ahead and stored in the freezer.

The first job was to make and chill the dough. Never work with warm pie dough. The next step was to scale off the dough and get everything together: pie pans filled with dough—six on each sheet pan—and then carried down the narrow steps into the basement to where the pie press was located. The crusts were pressed one at a time (about fifteen seconds each). This large machine had a big arm on it that cranked down with different heads on it for various sized pies—eight inches, nine inches and a little tart shell. The press was plugged in to heat up the heads so that they pre-baked the pie shells. After pressing, the pie pans were put back on the sheet pan and carried back up the steep steps. I hated that job because it took all night to make about two hundred of them.

Then all the fillings had to be made: fruits, syrups and custards. Syrups are technically custards, but so as not to confuse we'll call them syrups.

On pie day, I would put everything together and bake them off. I had to have the first batch ready for the oven by 4:00 a.m. in order to get everything out by 7:30 a.m. Pies took a lot of time because everything had to be hand cut. The people I remember making most of them were Carl, Howard and me. Maybe it was considered a higher art form. I'd pick out the nicest ones for the orders. The others were put out in the cases, and even though not perfect, they sold anyway.

Except for the moments I'd run back and help with butter bits in between pies, the two days before Thanksgiving that's all I did—make three to four hundred pies. Sometimes I really miss that pace.

One of my strongest memories of Thanksgiving is the order placed by a church in Winton Place. They used Virginia Bakery pies for the dessert at their congregation's Thanksgiving meal. They alone ordered about two hundred pies. We had pie safes, boxes about two feet tall with eleven shelves in them. We'd pack them with pies, lock the front door with a pin, pack them in the van, a 1958 Ford Rambler, and hope for the best as the pies shifted around in the back going down the winding Clifton Avenue hill. The church members would then give us the best Thanksgiving dinner possible—the whole nine yards: two sheet pans full of delicious food. After the long hours we'd put in, we'd go home, eat and crash.

PIE DOUGH

2 Tbs. sugar
1 tsp. salt
5 oz. cold water
3½ cups pastry (winter) flour (all-purpose flour will work if you can't find winter)
4 oz. shortening
3 oz. butter

Dissolve the salt and sugar in the cold water.
Place the flour in a large bowl and add the shortening and butter.
Pie dough is a hands-on thing. Work the mix between your fingertips until you have pellets the size of peas.

Once you have the pellets, make a well or hole in the center and wash your hands.
Stir and dump the sugar, salt and water mixture and pour it in the well.
Draw the flour in with the rubber spatula from the sides and mix until just incorporated. You could use your hands to finish mixing, but I find it better at home to finish with a rubber spatula.
Dump onto a floured pan, dust the top lightly with flour and shape into a rectangle.

What you are trying to do when mixing is make little pellets by surrounding little pieces of fat with flour. When your dough is rolled out, this trapped fat will form flat pockets in the dough. When baked, this fat will produce steam and give the dough its characteristic flakiness. This is why it is important not to overwork pie dough. If the fat gets totally incorporated into the flour, you will lose this flakiness. If you've done it right, you will see little pockets of fat in the dough.

Chill dough in the refrigerator at least one hour.

Your dough is made. You can store it covered in the fridge for several days, and it also freezes well. If you want, you can divide it into two 12-oz. pieces, which is what you'll use to make pie shells.

When you are ready to make pies, pull the dough pieces needed from the fridge and let them approach room temperature for about thirty minutes. Open-faced pies require one 12-oz. piece; covered pies require two pieces—one for the bottom and one for the top crust.

> Many cookbooks say besides chilling the fat, the time in the refrigerator also lets the gluten relax, producing a softer dough.
>
> The temperature of the dough is the critical part. If the dough is too cold, you will have to overwork it when rolling, and the trapped fat will get mashed into the flour. If the dough is too warm, the fat will mix with the flour with the same result. The trick is to have the temperature just right so the fat forms layers between the flour. You will see this as you roll the dough.

Using a rolling pin and lots of flour, roll the bottom piece on a floured board to a size about one inch bigger around the edges than your pie pan.

Dust the flour off the dough and place the piece in the pie pan. The dough should hang over the edges.

Press the dough into the pan and trim the excess with the side of your hand, or you could use a knife.

Egg wash the edge, which will help seal the top to the bottom. If you are making an open-faced pie, you can skip this step.

SYRUP PIES

Syrup pies use partially baked pie shells.

Roll out one 12-oz. piece of pie dough (see recipe on page 170) one inch bigger than your pan.

Press the dough into the pan and trim the excess with the side of your hand, or you could use a knife. Fill the shell with baking beads.

Preheat oven to 425 degrees.

Bake for approximately 15 minutes in oven. The temperature and time given is based on blind baking, as described on page 173, with the weighted beads that conduct the heat evenly and slowly.

Let cool. You can now fill your shell with the syrup filling and bake.

> Technically, these are custard pies, as they use eggs as the thickening agent. These were my favorite pies because they used a par-baked shell and a pre-made filling. On Thanksgiving morning, all I had to do was pull the shells from the freezer, pour in the filling and bake. These were always the first pies in the oven. I would make the fruit pies while these were baking.

CHESS PIE FILLING

1 1/2 cups sugar
1/4 tsp. salt
2 Tbs. pastry flour
5 oz. (1/2 cup + 2 Tbs.) egg yolks
1 12-oz. can evaporated milk
1/2 tsp. vanilla
3 oz. shortening
2 oz. butter

Combine sugar, salt and flour.
Add egg yolks and mix.
Add milk and vanilla.
Melt shortening and butter and add them to other ingredients.
Mix well and pour in a par-baked pie shell.

> The guys at the firehouse loved the chess pies. They would send their scouts over to see what time the pies would be out.

Preheat oven to 350 degrees.

Place a baking sheet on lower rack to catch any juices that might drip while baking.

Place pie on upper rack of oven and bake for approximately 1 hour. You want a nice golden crust.

> At the bakery, we had the heated pie press that would not only form the crimped edge but would partially bake the dough. You can accomplish this at home by lining the shell with parchment paper and then covering it with glass or ceramic baking beads made for this purpose. Doing this will prevent the dough on the bottom from puffing up or shrinking and the dough on the sides from sliding down or collapsing. Remove beads after shell has cooled. This is called blind baking.

PECAN PIE FILLING

1 cup sugar
¼ tsp. salt
3 eggs
1 cup corn syrup
2 Tbs. melted butter
½ tsp. vanilla
3 cups whole pecan pieces

Combine sugar, salt and eggs. Add corn syrup, then melted butter and vanilla.

The mixture can be used now or stored in the fridge.

To make the pie, place the whole pecan pieces in the partially baked shell and pour the filling over it.

Preheat oven to 350 degrees.

Bake for approximately 1 hour. You want a nice golden crust.

All the syrup pies are baked in a 350-degree oven so the custard will set before the tops burn. Baking these pies can be tricky because they don't look done when they are done. They usually take at least one hour. The center will still be soft and jiggly when the pie is done. The carry-over heat will set the center. I would bake the pies until the tops had a nice color and pray that the centers would set. They always did. Be careful when removing the pies from the oven, as the centers will be soft and they can be hard to handle. Use a baking or pizza peel if you have one. Cool on a rack until set.

CUSTARD PIES

Custard pies use pre-baked pie shells. Roll out one 12-oz. piece of pie dough (see recipe on page 170) one inch bigger than your pan.

Press the dough onto the back of a pan and trim the excess with the side of your hand, or you could use a knife. Poke a few small holes in the dough with a fork to allow steam to escape. Preheat oven to 400 degrees.

Bake 15 to 20 minutes until golden. Allow to cool before filling the shell with the custard.

It helps if you have two different-sized pie pans, one just slightly smaller than the other. Turn the smaller pan upside down on a baking sheet. Put the rolled-out dough over it and trim the edges. Poke the small holes. You will be baking the dough on the bottom side of the smaller pan. When done, carefully flip the baked shell into the larger pie pan.

CUSTARD PIE FILLING

6 Tbs. cornstarch
2 cups cold milk
¾ cup sugar
⅛ tsp. salt
6 egg yolks
3 egg whites
½ tsp. vanilla
3 Tbs. sugar

Dissolve cornstarch in ½ cup of the milk.

Combine remaining milk, sugar, salt and egg yolks in a heavy saucepan and carefully heat to boiling, stirring often.

As soon as mixture boils, add dissolved cornstarch and cook until thick.

Remove from heat and cool, stirring occasionally.

Meanwhile, whip the egg whites and vanilla until stiff.

Gradually fold in sugar.

When the custard is cooler but still warm, fold in the egg whites and blend well.

Fill a pre-baked pie shell and top the pie with whipped cream.

Allow time for filling to set. Let cool at room temperature before cutting or refrigerating.

COCONUT CUSTARD PIE

Follow directions above and add 1 cup of coconut to the custard at the end.

BANANA CUSTARD PIE

Follow directions above and add 1½ cup of sliced bananas to the custard at the end.

You can also use a prepared crust from the store. A chocolate crust goes great with the banana cream pie. Use graham for the plain and coconut.

CHOCOLATE CUSTARD PIE

Follow directions above, adding 6 Tbs. of cocoa powder and cutting back on the starch to 3 Tbs.

Doughnuts

Doughnuts—"sinkers," "crullers," "gaskets," "cop cookies," "packzi," "dunkers," "yum-yums." Call them what you will, they are America's most popular breakfast item. People have tried the commercial breakfast sandwiches and the smoothie bars, but bakers everywhere know that doughnuts are the breakfast of choice.

Doughnut work started very early. At 1:00 a.m., the baker in charge of doughnuts started his day in order to have the cases stocked by opening time. The doughnut fryer was downstairs, so he had to make up the doughnuts, take them down the steps and fry them and then bring them back up so they could be packed and sold. People loved being able to stop in on the fly and grab a warm, fresh doughnut—very light, very good.

Helen Adams shared, "When my kids were in grade school, my husband started a tradition of Doughnut Friday. They would stop on the way to school for a fresh Virginia Bakery doughnut. Virginia Bakery was the quintessential old-fashioned neighborhood bakery. It is sorely missed."

James Bender shared that sentiment when he said, "It was a sad day when we were no longer able to buy those wonderful creations, glorious doughnuts, especially the glazed yeast." Others spoke about the jelly-filled doughnuts as being better than good, the best, and how they enjoyed biting into them and having delicious jelly squirt out. But the doughnut that received the most rave reviews from all the people who shared memories was the masterpiece known as the Virginia reel.

General Doughnut Information

At first, I didn't want to include doughnuts in this book because I thought they were too hard to make at home. After playing with them and doing some online research, I found they were easier than I had believed.

One of the obstacles was the deep fryer, which proved to have an easy solution. I went online and found several "Doughnut Making Machines" that ranged in price from $61 to over $12,000. You can buy a lot of doughnuts for $12,000. Frugal as I am, I settled on a deep twelve-inch cast-iron skillet purchased at Goodwill for $10. Add $5 worth of frying shortening and you have a $15 doughnut fryer.

A frying thermometer is extremely helpful, as doughnuts are temperature dependent. If the oil is too hot, the outside will burn before the center batter/dough is cooked. If you've ever had a real greasy doughnut, the oil was too cold. If the oil is just right (365 degrees), a nice crust will form, preventing further oil absorption, and the doughnut will cook slowly enough to cook the center.

Doughnut frying is a real art gained only with several flips of the doughnut sticks. It takes a little practice but is really fun once you get the hang of it. I did the doughnuts for a couple of years while I was going to UC. I'd get in at 1:00 a.m., have the doughnuts ready for the store by 7:30, go to my 8:00 classes and then come back, clean up and get ready for the next day.

One thing I did find online that I found useful are the handheld doughnut droppers. We called them hoppers. Whereas the yeast doughnuts are hand formed, you need to have a hopper to drop cake doughnuts and Virginia reels. They sell both the plain hopper for cake doughnuts and the "twisted" reel hopper. Good news for home doughnut fiends.

When frying doughnuts, the shortening/oil combination is ideally half and half, but any combo will work. You want oils/fats with a high smoking point.

Be prepared—a grease fire is always possible when heating large amounts of oil. Know how to put one out before you start.
1. Always use a dry chemical extinguisher.
2. Never aim the extinguisher directly at the source of the fire; rather, start in a circular motion around the flames, which will remove the oxygen and the fire will diminish. Then you can hit it directly.
3. Fire will go out!

"What are we supposed to do when we want a Virginia reel?" asked Alice Derrick. Tim Lanham echoed the thought behind that question: "I haven't found anyone that makes them as good since or, for that matter, makes them at all. I understand it's a labor-intensive doughnut and most bakeries don't want to mess with trying to make the twisted doughnut in the shape of a ring, deep fried with a very light, almost airy texture. Oh my, they were delicious and to this day my favorite. One of their doughnuts, a cold glass of milk and all was right with the world."

Brian Messmore, an EMT who started working in Cincinnati in 1985, was at the bakery all the time. "Our station was at Marshall and McMicken, and we'd stop in most mornings. There was an older lady who was in her eighties [Myrtle Thie], and she really liked me. She'd always slip me an extra doughnut and give me that ornery wink. I would tease her and tell her to call me later so we could 'go out and cut a rug,' which is what my grandma used to say about dancing. When I walked out the door and looked back at her, she'd be laughing and throw her hand at me to get out."

Bill Pritz, a baker with a high regard for Virginia Bakery products, summed up the topic by saying they always made the best doughnuts in town.

Yeast Doughnuts

For yeast doughnuts, use a 12-oz. piece of yellow dough (see page 109).
Divide the dough into six balls, each weighing 2 oz.
Place the dough balls on a floured pan and cover with a light cloth.
Proof in a warm spot until doubled.

Take the dough ball and, using your fingertips, make a hole in the center and roll the dough inward until you have a nice smooth doughnut. Practice; you'll get it.
Proof the doughnut lightly covered with the cloth until doubled.

Our doughnuts were not cut, but hand shaped.

When frying, heat at least 2" of a shortening/oil combination to 365 degrees in a wide skillet.
Drop the doughnuts into hot fat, leaving room for expansion.

Don't do too many at a time or your temperature may fall too low, giving you greasy doughnuts.

When they are brown on one side, use chopsticks or the ends of wooden spoons to flip the doughnuts over.

When done, remove to rack to drain and cool until you can handle them.

Yeast doughnuts can be served plain, glazed, dipped in chocolate (use a thinned ganache—see page 139) or rolled in powdered or cinnamon sugar.

If glazing (see page 140), do so while still hot.

If sugaring, allow doughnuts to cool slightly or the hot oil will dissolve the sugar.

Yield: 6 doughnuts

CRULLERS

¾ cup sugar
⅛ tsp. salt
3 Tbs. honey
4 egg yolks
3 Tbs. melted butter

½ cup + 2 Tbs. milk
¼ tsp. lemon extract
3 cups winter flour
1 Tbs. baking powder
¼ tsp. nutmeg

Cream the first five ingredients.
Add the milk and lemon extract and scrape bowl.
Combine remaining dry ingredients and add to bowl.
Mix until combined, scraping the bowl if necessary.
Turn dough onto a floured board and form a rectangle about 12" tall and 9" wide.
Cut the crullers into 1½" x 3" rectangles.
Give them one twist like a candy cane and put them on a floured pan until ready to fry.

Follow the frying directions given for the yeast doughnuts.
The crullers were either plain or glazed
If glazing (see page 140), do so while still hot.

Yield: 24 crullers

Virginia Reels—"Reely just a sweet *Pâte à Choux*"

1 cup water
4 Tbs. shortening
1 Tbs. butter
1 cup bread flour
1½ Tbs. sugar
¼ tsp. salt
3 eggs
6 Tbs. warm milk

For this recipe, you will need a doughnut hopper that has a spiral head in order to make the doughnuts look like the ones sold in the bakery. If you don't have one of those, you can make them with a regular hopper or even a piping bag. They won't look the same, but they'll taste the same.

You will need a mixer with a metal bowl.
Place the first three ingredients in the metal bowl of your mixer and heat to boiling.

Combine flour, sugar and salt and pour into boiling mix.

Lower the heat and, with a wooden spoon, stir and cook dough until it forms a tight ball, about 1 minute.

Place bowl on mixer with the paddle attachment.

On medium speed add one egg at a time, incorporating well between each addition.

Add half the milk, scrape and mix.

Add remaining milk and repeat.

Fry the reels while the batter is still warm.

When frying, heat at least 2" of a shortening/oil combination to 365 degrees in a wide skillet.

Fill the hopper and drop the doughnuts into hot fat, leaving room for expansion.

Don't do too many at a time or your temperature may fall too low, giving you greasy doughnuts.

When they are brown on one side, use chopsticks or the ends of wooden spoons to flip the doughnuts over.

When done, remove to rack to drain and cool until you can handle them.

The Virginia reels were always glazed (see page 140) while still hot.

Yield: 1 dozen doughnuts

> Oh hot doughnut, Love of my morning. One of the best things I have ever tasted is a fresh hot glazed Virginia reel. "Glazed Sweet Air" is what I reverently call them. To get one, you either have to work in a bakery or make them at home. Those were my favorite, the doughnuts I had a weakness for.
>
> One time I fell asleep and burned my apron when making pâte à choux. I'd stand there forever when cooking that stuff. The smoke woke me up.

Cookies

Based on the number of times former customers mentioned receiving a cookie from the counter ladies when they were little, giving young children a tea cookie as a treat for coming in the bakery when their parents were shopping was probably one of the smartest marketing concepts that Virginia Bakery ever conceived of and used. And they continuously followed that tradition from 1927 through 2000, making long-lasting impressions on generations of customers. Men and women in their seventies and eighties reported that they remembered those treats as if it were yesterday. People have never forgotten that generosity, which for some, no doubt, played a part in their feeling of loyalty to the Thies and Virginia Bakery but for others may have had another importance. Judy Trombly Ganance shared that, on a rare occasion, she was invited behind the counter by one of the bakers to sample a cookie directly off one of the enormous sheet trays. "And when you're a kid, it all seemed so big and grand. While this memory is foggy, I do think it had a significant influence in my later years in becoming a baker/pastry chef."

According to the 1960 "Vitality News" merchandising feature, during a week's time Virginia Bakery carried more than thirty varieties of cookies, and the tea and party cookies sold extremely well. Janet Thie Koenig knows that Christmas cookies were big sellers. "We had everything in the world." While customers have the joyful memory of coming in and choosing from a large selection, the excitement wasn't always matched on the other side of the counter. While Jennifer Thie reported loving the Christmas cookies because of the variety, Ron Thie's comment was that while working there he "learned to hate cookies after standing there on a Sunday afternoon packing dozens after dozens of boxes." Janet remembers working with her mother and packing orders all night long. Around 6:00 a.m., Myrtle would say she couldn't do any more and would go to the upstairs apartment to get some sleep for a short while until the store opened and she'd start all over again. Karen Striet also remembers working in the bakery during the holiday rush, going in about 4:00 p.m. and working all night packing cookie orders. "P&G would order one thousand one-pound boxes. During these all-nighters, the young ones would be packing and the bakers would be baking. Around 5:00 a.m., someone would go down to Hopple Street and get White Castles."

Emily Scott wrote in her 2000 UC *News Record* article that the quantity of cookies made was astonishing. "During the 1999 holiday season, the bakery went through five tons of flour, two and a half tons of sugar and one ton of butter just to make their iced sugar cookies!"

For Tom Thie, cookies were a love/hate thing.

> *I hated them because they were so time consuming, required a lot of special high-priced ingredients (do you know how much a ton of pecans cost?) and posed special headaches for the order department. I loved them because it was one more thing that made us unique. I knew we were the only bakery in town that made such a variety of cookies completely from scratch—no pre-mixes or, worse, already baked cookies here. I was particularly proud of our cookies, especially at Christmas. People would fight over them. What better compliment? Oh yeah, the smiles of little children. A little face with a sugar-coated smile is a special treat. I miss that the most.*
>
> *Christmas to me meant schnecken and cookies, which we would start on the day after Thanksgiving. Literally, tons of dough were mixed and frozen. This is helpful for the baker; a lot of the work involved with cookies can be done ahead of time. Most cookie doughs freeze well. Our walk-ins were full by the first week of December.*
>
> *We made about fifty different cookies at Christmas. It was crazy from the day after Thanksgiving until December 24. Cookies were everywhere. We even used an apartment upstairs to pack and store orders.*

Whether during the holidays or other times of the year, Virginia Bakery cookies were in demand. Dennis Smith, a salesman serving the baking industry, stated that the cookies were really good and the bakery was known for catering to "the carriage trade." Many people reported that they have never found another bakery that can match those cookies. Susan Wood expressed this feeling when she said, "They're like gold. Others can look pretty, and I get excited, but they never taste the same." Susan Newmark said,

I always thought that Virginia Bakery had the best tasting tea cookies in the city. I recall being angry years ago when there was a piece by Chuck Martin in the Enquirer...*about the best Cincinnati tea cookies and Virginia Bakery was not mentioned. As an active baker, I trust that my taste in cookies was not off base and assumed he didn't know the quality here. The bakers made different cookies every day to keep them replenished. I found out the days...when they baked my favorites and tried to time my visits for those days! How could he not mention Virginia Bakery? Theirs were wonderful—full of taste like homemade butter cookies.*

Laurie Bredenfoerder added, "You know, every time I think about the Virginia Bakery, I wish I had a quarter-pound of tea cookies, in one of those crunchy white paper sacks, in my hand. I'd even welcome the powdered sugar streaks on my clothes!" Laurie was likely thinking of the Mexican wedding cookies when she wrote that, as were many of the other people who shared their memories. If the people who responded to the request for customer memories represent customers in general, then Mexican wedding cookies were definitely among the most popular cookies and hard to find anywhere else. Annie Glenn and Karen Striet remember "dipping" and tossing the cookies in the powdered sugar while the cookies were still warm from the oven so that the coating would stick, as well as filling the cases with them and being allowed to eat the broken ones. Barbara Weishar added the memory of weighing the cookies in the large scoop pan that was set on top of the scale. "When you had to pack a pound of cookies, you had to put them in and lay them in the pound box just right."

Among the other most remembered cookies were the butter nests, which were available with a variety of colored icing centers and edgings. A nest cookie, for example, could have a pink, yellow or white dollop at Easter, while the same nest cookies might have orange-colored or dark chocolate centers at Halloween. Sometimes the edges were rolled in chopped nuts, other times multicolored nonpareils or chocolate Jimmies. Mark Leathers made an interesting and unusual comment when describing how much he loved these cookies:

Virginia Bakery taught me what junk food was! Not because the tasty treats at Virginia Bakery were junk, but because everything else paled by comparison. The quality and genuine ingredients were apparent. When I had a cookie from Virginia Bakery, it melted in my mouth and left a wonderful aftertaste. Other cookies and supermarket "treats" could never compare. Years later, when I was on my own and could literally buy anything I wanted at the grocery, I realized after chasing way too many calories that a package of Oreos or Little Debbie may be cheap and easily available, but they were like plastic and greasy substitutes for real baked goods…The little dough cookies with the huge dollop of chocolate icing—how I looked forward to those each year. I would find them at all our parties…That gold of my childhood, the little dough cookie with the chocolate! I would nibble around the sides, gnawing away the plain cookie, knowing that the treasure I sought was in the middle, that sweet chocolate blob!…No matter how many I had, I still wanted more, and nearly fifty years later, I still do.

The following pages are a dream come true for cookie lovers, containing recipes for eleven of the most popular cookies sold at the Virginia Bakery, including some of the cookies mentioned above, as well as Moe's date-nut kiss, which during the 1990s was chosen by thirteen TriState bakers as one of their favorite Christmas cookies. Imagine standing in front of the case and pointing to the cookies you want. You can once again enjoy the goodness.

General Cookie Information

Mixing
Most cookie doughs follow the basic creaming method. One important thing to remember is not to over-mix cookie dough; just bring it together. Don't play with the dough on the bench either. Handle as little as possible. This keeps them tender by not over-mixing the gluten.

Creaming
It's easy. Using a mixer, cream sugar, salt and fats. Add and cream liquids. Add remaining dry ingredients and bring together. For example, nest cookies: cream sugar, salt, butter and shortening. Add eggs and vanilla. Scrape bowl and cream. Add flour and mix just until combined. Simple.

Storing Dough

Most cookie doughs can be stored for several days refrigerated or months frozen. Actually, cookie dough should rest in the refrigerator at least one hour before using. The exception would be the doughs that are "bagged"/piped. In those cases, they should rest at room temperature. The resting period gives the dough time to homogenize, makes it easier to handle and definitely affects the baking. I've noticed that fresh doughs will spread too much during baking and you'll wind up with a cracker. Make sure they are well covered with plastic to prevent drying.

Pans

Put cookie pucks (disks of dough) on parchment-lined half-sheet pans. Leave room for cookies that spread.

Baking

Cookies bake better when the dough is cold. You can even put your panned cookies in the fridge before baking if it's too hot in the kitchen. Keep your cookies uniform so they all bake at the same time. PULL YOUR COOKIES OUT OF THE OVEN BEFORE THEY ARE DONE. Cookies are extremely prone to carry-over baking. They will continue to brown even after you pull them out of the oven. Cookies are the hardest item to bake. Too soon and they're raw and crumble. Too late and oh well, they're burnt.

It takes an experienced oven man to bake cookies all day. That was all he did—put cookies in and out of the oven. One or two minutes either way could mean hundreds of lost dollars. I won't give you definite times on cookies, although about eight minutes is close for small cookies. Bake them at 375 degrees until they just start to brown around the edges. Pull and cool on the pan and they should be perfect. Cool the baking sheet after it's been in the oven and before putting the next batch in. While one pan is baking, the other can be put in the refrigerator.

Storing Cookies

Store, using airtight containers, as soon as cool because cookies go stale quickly. We would just wrap whole pans in clear plastic bags.

NESTS

¾ cup sugar
¼ tsp. salt
¾ cup shortening
½ cup butter
1 egg
½ tsp. vanilla
3¼ cups winter flour (all-purpose flour will work if you can't find winter)

Additional ingredients needed: your choice of chopped nuts or decorettes and icing (see pages 139 and 143)

Place parchment paper on baking sheets.

Follow basic creaming method (see page 186).
Do *not* refrigerate dough before rolling in coatings.
Put your choice of coating (chopped nuts, multicolored nonpareils or chocolate Jimmies) in a glass baking dish.
Take a handful of dough and roll into a cylinder about 1½" in diameter.
Roll the dough in the baking dish to coat the outside of the cylinder. You may need to press slightly. Keep the cylinder round.
Place the dough cylinders on a parchment-lined baking sheet and refrigerate until firm.
Cut the chilled cookie dough in ½" slices and lay on their sides (so the coating is around the outside rims) about 1" apart on a parchment-lined cookie sheet. Stagger the rows to allow for more cookies.
Pan all the cookies and then go back and press your thumb in the center of each cookie to form a "nest" to hold the icing after baking.
Preheat oven to 375 degrees.
Place baking sheet on upper rack and bake for approximately 8 minutes until just brown around the edges.
After the cookies cool, put a dot of colored icing or chocolate in the center.

Yield: 6 dozen cookies

MOON CRESCENTS

These were among the bakers' least favorite cookies and were saved for "The Mixer," usually the highest position on the totem pole in the back shop. This helped to keep him humble. A lot of times this was me. When piping this many cookies, well, let's just say your arm gets really sore. After a while you start to develop a "Popeye" arm and possible tennis elbow from constantly contracting that tendon in your elbow. My arm is finally back to normal.

There was an enormous amount of squeezing going on, but these had an added twist. If "The Mixer" wasn't careful in breaking down the almond paste and sugar into a smooth paste, lumps would remain and often clog the pastry bag. You would have to stop, clean out the bag, unclog the tip, refill the bag and start over. A pain in the keister and, like roaches, where there is one, there's usually more. This was also a good reason to save these cookies for "The Mixer." If he screwed up the mix, he paid the price.

1 lb. almond paste
¾ cup sugar
¼ tsp. salt
¾ cup egg whites
1¼ cups shortening
¾ cup butter
½ tsp. lemon extract
3 cups winter flour (all-purpose flour will also work)

Additional ingredients needed: chocolate icing (see page 139) or raspberry jelly.

Place parchment paper on baking sheets.
Cream the almond paste, sugar and salt until well combined.
Add the egg whites slowly to make a smooth paste.
Add the shortening, butter and lemon extract and cream well.
Mix in the flour.

Using a pastry bag, pipe the dough in the shape of a small crescent onto the parchment-lined baking pan.

Preheat oven to 375 degrees.

Place baking sheet on upper rack and bake for approximately 8 minutes until just brown around the edges.

After the cookies cool, the crescents are made into sandwich cookies: two cookies put together with a filling. The crescents were filled with chocolate icing or raspberry jelly. The jelly crescents were dusted with powdered sugar.

Yield: approximately 8 dozen cookies

Mexican Wedding Cookies

¾ cup sugar
¼ tsp. salt
1 cup shortening
5 Tbs. butter
½ tsp. vanilla
3¼ cups winter flour (all-purpose flour will also work)
1¼ cups pecan pieces

Additional ingredient needed: 1½ cup of powdered sugar for coating

Follow basic creaming method (see page 186), adding nuts last.
Do *not* refrigerate dough at this stage.
Roll dough into 1½" diameter log.
Refrigerate for a half hour to an hour.
Cut cylinder of dough into ¼" thick disks.
Preheat oven to 375 degrees.
Place baking sheet on upper rack and bake for approximately 8 minutes until just brown around the edges.
When cool, roll/toss the cookies in powdered sugar.

Yield: approximately 10 dozen cookies

SHORTBREAD DOUGH

1 large egg
½ cup sugar
2½ cups winter flour (all-purpose flour will also work)
⅛ tsp. baking powder
¼ tsp. salt
¼ tsp. lemon extract
½ cup shortening
½ cup butter

Shortbread dough is probably the most versatile cookie dough, as several cookies can be made from the same base dough. Shortbread sugar cutouts were the most popular. They came as stars, hearts, Christmas trees, shamrocks, Easter eggs, pumpkins, etc. All were topped with colored sugar.

This cookie recipe does *not* follow the creaming method.
Start by whipping the egg and sugar (at medium speed) until fluffy with the paddle attachment.
Add flour, baking powder, salt and lemon extract.
Scrape bowl well and mix by stirring.
Cut in shortening and butter a little at a time, but do not over mix.
Refrigerate before using.

SHORTBREAD SUGAR CUTOUTS

On a floured surface, roll the dough to a thickness of ¼".
Cut with a cookie cutter.
Place on parchment-lined cookie sheet.
Brush the cookies lightly with egg wash to moisten—if the cookies get too wet, the sugar will dissolve.
Cover with colored sugar.
Preheat oven to 375 degrees.
Place baking sheet on upper rack and bake lightly for approximately 8 minutes until just brown around the edges.

Yield: 2 to 4 dozen cookies, depending on shape of cutter

CASHEW HALF MOONS

shortbread dough (see page 191)
1 cup of small cashew pieces
$\frac{1}{2}$ cup of granulated sugar

On a floured surface, roll the dough $\frac{1}{4}$"
thick and form/cut a square shape.
Egg wash the surface lightly.
Cover with cashew pieces.

Sprinkle the cashews with the granulated sugar.
Cut the dough in columns, using a round cookie cutter (held at an angle) to cut out a $\frac{1}{4}$ section of the circle creating a crescent shape. (See diagram.)
Place on parchment-lined cookie sheet.
Preheat oven to 375 degrees.
Place baking sheet on upper rack and bake lightly for approximately 8 minutes until just brown around the edges.

Yield: approximately 4 dozen cookies

Cutting Crescents

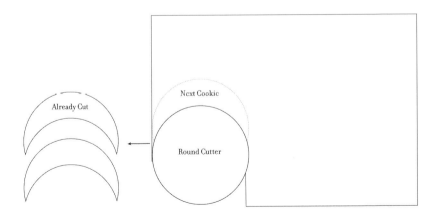

Already Cut

Next Cookie

Round Cutter

FRENCH MACAROONS

shortbread dough (see page 191)
almond paste topping (see below)
½ cup of raspberry jam

On a floured surface, roll the dough ¼" thick.

Cut dough with a 2" round ruffled cookie cutter.

Place on parchment-lined cookie sheet.

Squeeze a ring of almond paste topping around the edge on top of the dough disk and put a dot of raspberry jam in the center.

Preheat oven to 375 degrees.

Place baking sheet on upper rack and bake lightly for approximately 8 minutes until just brown around the edges.

Yield: approximately 6 dozen cookies

Almond Paste Topping

2 oz. almond paste
¼ cup sugar
pinch of salt
½ egg white
⅛ tsp. vanilla

Cream almond paste, sugar and salt.
Mix egg white and vanilla. Combine with fork until whites loosen.
Add enough to make a stiff paste that you can still pipe through a pastry tip.

DAY AND NIGHT COOKIES

> This is my daughter's favorite.

Shortbread dough (see page 191)
1½ cups of chocolate pieces for melting

On a floured surface, roll the dough ¼"
thick.
Cut dough with a 3" round cookie cutter.
Place on parchment-lined cookie sheet.
Preheat oven to 375 degrees.
Place baking sheet on upper rack and
bake lightly for approximately 8 minutes
until just brown around the edges.
When cool, dip half of the face of the
cookie in your favorite melted chocolate.

Yield: approximately 3 dozen cookies

SUGAR COOKIES

1 cup sugar
¼ tsp. salt
¼ cup shortening
¼ cup butter
1 Tbs. of stirred egg
½ tsp. vanilla
1½ cups winter flour (all-purpose will work if you can't find winter flour)
⅛ tsp. nutmeg

Follow basic creaming method (see page 186).
After mixing, refrigerate dough for an hour rest.
On a floured surface, roll dough into logs and cut into pieces the size you can
form into 1" diameter balls.

Press each ball into granulated sugar, flattening slightly as you go.

Turn puck (disk of dough) over and place on a parchment-lined cookie sheet, leaving plenty of room to spread. These will be about 4" round when done.

Preheat oven to 375 degrees.

Place baking sheet on upper rack and bake lightly for approximately 8 minutes until edges begin to turn brown.

Yield: approximately 4 dozen cookies

BRANDY BUMPS

½ cup light brown sugar
¼ tsp. salt
2 Tbs. shortening
2 Tbs. butter
1 extra large egg
½ tsp. brandy flavor
1 cup bread flour
1 tsp. baking soda
⅛ tsp. powdered cloves
¼ tsp. nutmeg
½ tsp. cinnamon
¼ tsp. salt
1 ½ cups chopped candied cherries
½ cup chopped candied pineapple
¾ cup raisins
1 cup pecan pieces

This was my favorite Christmas cookie, and I always made sure to "test" the first batch. You'll see what I mean.

Follow basic creaming method (see page 186).

Combine first four ingredients.

Add egg and brandy.

Combine next six dry ingredients and add.

Fold in fruit and nuts.

Place dough by the tablespoon on parchment-lined cookie sheet with just a little distance between them.

Preheat oven to 375 degrees.

Place baking sheet on upper rack and bake lightly for approximately 8 minutes.

Yield: approximately 6 dozen cookies

DATE NUT KISSES

I used to hate these cookies because I had to grind the dates and pecans together in a hand grinder. After we bought the Cusinarts, I didn't mind them so much.

1 cup pecans
1½ cups dates
egg whites from 2 eggs
¼ tsp. vanilla
1 cup sugar
⅛ tsp. salt

Grind pecans and dates together into small pieces. Don't overdo it or you will make a paste that's hard to mix in.
Whip egg whites and vanilla at high speed to soft peaks.
Gradually fold in sugar and salt.
Place in mixing bowl and fold in date/pecan mixture.
Grease hands and drop on parchment-lined baking sheet in the form of kisses by pinching between the tips of your fingers.
Preheat oven to 375 degrees.
Place baking sheet on upper rack and bake lightly for approximately 8 minutes.

Yield: approximately 4 dozen cookies

ALMOND CROISSANTS

1 cup sugar
1 cup almond paste
⅛ tsp. salt
2 Tbs. flour
1 egg white
½ cup chopped cherry pieces
½ cup pecan pieces
Additional small pecan pieces to roll in

Combine first four ingredients.

Gradually add egg white.

Gently mix in cherries and pecans.

Cut dough into 1" round pieces.

Roll in pecans to make a 3" log.

Bend the log in the shape of a crescent and place on parchment-lined baking sheet.

Preheat oven to 375 degrees.

Place baking sheet on upper rack and bake lightly for approximately 8 minutes until lightly browned. While still warm, brush with glaze (see page 142).

Yield: approximately 4 dozen cookies

Aunt Sandy's favorite.

Breads

B read, often called the "Staple of Life," was a regularly baked and sold item at Virginia Bakery. For many people, a trip to the Ludlow Avenue shopping district always included a stop into Virginia Bakery for a fresh loaf. As Hattie Thie told reporter Willard Clopton in 1961, "Homemade bread goes big." In June 2000, in an article for the *News Record*, the University of Cincinnati student newspaper, Emily Scott wrote, "If you're not a sweet lover, Virginia Bakery has some of the best bread in Cincinnati. Their bread is made from scratch and baked all day long." That baked-from-scratch flavor and delicious aroma brought folks back time after time, in some instances invoking memories of the bread their mothers and grandmothers used to make. Phrases such as "absolutely the best bread," "no one ever made better," "their bread has never been duplicated" and "I can't find bread like that anywhere" came up repeatedly in the letters and phone calls we received.

In a 1960 General Mills "Vitality News" Merchandising Feature article, Virginia Bakery was reported as offering, during an average week, fifteen to twenty different kinds of bread. In that same piece, Bill Thie noted an increase in the sale of "hard rolls and French bread, largely because people now know how to use such specialty breads and rolls in different and unusual sandwiches." By the mid-1980s, Virginia Bakery was making and selling over fifty bread and roll varieties. The basic breads, such as homemade white, buttercrust and wheat, were made daily. Over the years, depending on the time of day, bakers were likely to be seen through the window that overlooked

The Thie bakers started young. Little Bill with a loaf of French bread. *Photographed by John C. Murphy.*

the parking lot as they worked on the bread dough. In addition to the basic breads, each day of the week a specialty bread was offered. On cheese bread day, Bill would be covered in a golden cheese color.

Most families had a Virginia Bakery routine. The trip was often weekly; for some, the bakery odyssey would occur a couple of times a week; and, for others, even more frequently. Oftentimes ladies who lived right up the street would walk to the store every day, and children would be sent daily on their bikes to get a loaf of bread and something for dessert. If they got there just before closing, the large loaves might have been sold out and they would have to settle for a small one. (There were little postage stamp–sized labels that were baked onto the bottom of the loaves indicating their weight/size. The labels were laid in the lined-up pans, with writing side down, before the dough was put into the pans.)

For many, the plan was to arrive at the bakery at their favorite time: the moment the fresh loaves were hot from the oven. This would have been in the afternoon, because traditionally breads were the last thing to be taken out of the ovens each day. If customers arrived before the breads were out, the shop girls would run to the back and ask "the guys" for a time. Once the bread was out of the oven, the bakers would bring the loaves down to the front of the store straight from the rack.

Customers still have lasting memories of the wonderful aromas as the bakers pulled the hot baked breads from the rotating oven, a smell that can't be matched by bread bought in a grocery store. The loaves would come out whole and warm, and if they weren't too hot, the ladies behind the counter would ask customers if they'd like their bread sliced. Annie Glenn shared, "Some of the breads (especially the buttercrust) would be so hot and fragile when they came directly from the oven. If a customer wanted it sliced hot, we used one of the two (ancient/classic) bread-slicers (one was a thin slicer). The bread would collapse when it was that hot. And the wax bags we wrapped

If you recognize these pictures, you remember how noisy the slicer was and how the loaves of bread had stamps on the bottoms.

them in would steam and be very hot to handle!" Some families remembered that while the outer wax bags would be warm, the inner plastic bags had to be left open because otherwise condensation would form. On such occasions, the shop ladies might tell customers that the bread was just too hot to slice and they would have to take it home as a whole loaf; but more often than not, they could be captivated as the shop ladies placed their loaves on the back side of the reliable, noisy machine by the window and they watched the bread vibrate forward through the sharp slicer. Following that, the bread was quickly and efficiently lifted and placed on a V-shaped rack attached to the window ledge by the side of the slicer, which allowed the ladies to easily slip a bag over the sliced loaf. There were some families, however, who preferred bread whole so that they could cut the pieces as thick as they wanted.

Mark Leathers, one of Cindy Thie's nephews, represented many, many folks when he stated that what he loved about Virginia Bakery's breads was not just the aroma that stood out but also the buttery flavor, the good-to-bite-into texture and the old-fashioned appeal. A multitude of people admitted that the aroma of the freshly baked bread overtook them. "Forced" to reach into the bags and grab some slices, they were unable to get home without eating samples of the loaves—even if they lived only three minutes away. The only rationale for waiting until they reached home was the love of adding creamy butter on the warm bread. Janet Fast Andress shared a charming story from her childhood:

> *My most vivid memory occurred at the time my dear friend, Barbara Skinner Johns, and I were asked to buy a loaf of bread at the bakery. We felt very grown-up with the responsibility, but on the way home the mouthwatering aroma proved too tempting, so we pulled some tiny bites out of the bottom of the crust. Before we knew it, we had nibbled all the soft inside. So, sheepishly we delivered an empty shell of crust behind some snickers and giggles. Fortunately, our only punishment was to walk down Hosea Avenue again and buy another loaf of bread with our own money.*

While those two girls apparently loved the soft center of the bread, other families preferred the crusty portions. Joyzell George wrote, "My mom, dad, four brothers and I would fight over who would get the heels because that was the best part of the bread. Our treat would be to butter the bread and put it under the broiler and toast it—delicious."

"We never ate grocery bread" was almost a mantra among Virginia Bakery regulars. Some reported that while growing up they never experienced the very white and soft squishy store-bought bread. And many of them introduced their wives and husbands to what good bread was after they married.

Speaking of quality bread, there's one aspect of Virginia Bakery that is not well known—the fact that Tom worked with a cancer patient to create an iodine-free bread that she was able to eat. Debbi Hill wrote:

> *January 1991 brought the diagnosis of thyroid cancer. As a thirty-nine-year-old mother of two young children, this was not welcome news. The only effective treatment was radioactive iodine, which only worked if the patient went off medications and on a very strict and no-iodine diet for several months. The diet was extremely limiting, and the "bread" part of the food chain was my favorite one! Only one bakery in town made bread without iodine—*

Virginia Bakery. Every year before the diet began, there I would be loading up on my permitted number of slices for the length of the diet. The loaves were prepared for my freezer and clearly marked so no other family member would take even one precious slice! The diet and lack of medication would guarantee my energy level would be nonexistent quickly and another trip to the Clifton bakery not possible. Every evening, one slice of this delicious bread would be toasted. It was my treat for getting through another day without my medication. There was no question of cheating on this diet—it was saving my life. Five years later, the cancer was in remission. If it ever comes back, I'll be calling Tom Thie for help once again!

In a whole new way, Tom is now helping all of us. By using his recipes on the following pages, we can provide our families with five of Virginia Bakery's outstanding favorite breads. According to customers' comments, with the homemade white we will have the best toasting bread imaginable, as well as the basis for some outstanding Thanksgiving stuffing. Many people's all-time most favorite was the "beautiful golden" buttercrust bread that you will discover is ready to eat without adding anything. With the 100 percent whole wheat bread, we will derive the benefits for which many doctors (from Holmes Hospital) sent their patients to Virginia Bakery—they wanted them off "gummy grocery bread" and instead to eat healthy bread with no chemical preservatives. The list goes on. All the breads were good. Happy bread baking!

General Bread Information

A lot of bakeries feel the step of making a sponge is no longer necessary with the new and improved strains of yeast, and they are probably right. The sponge was originally used to make sure the yeast was spread evenly throughout the mixture, as well as to cultivate it. Actually, I'm willing to bet the first sponge occurred accidentally, as did the first beer and wine. Someone probably left a bit of grain and some water, possibly from making unleavened bread, and some natural yeast floating around in the air decided this would be a good place to make camp. Not wanting to waste the mixture, they baked with it anyway, regardless of the strange bubbles. Voila—yeast bread was born.

I think the sponge is essential. Customers always ask why our baked goods have a better flavor, and I am certain the sponge accounts for part of this. I've tried to skip this step and use the straight bread method. Believe me, the customers know. You won't find that recipe here.

If you look at a "regular" loaf of bread and a sponge-made loaf, you can see the difference. The regular loaf has very small air pockets and is soft enough to wad in a ball. On vacation in Michigan, my grandfather Bill used to take Wonder bread and mash it into a ball. "I wonder what's in it," he'd say, as he bounced it off the kitchen floor. "That's not bread," was his final condemnation. A sponge-made bread will have larger air pockets, giving it a lighter texture yet making it firm enough to butter as toast straight from the toaster. If you have tried that with regular bread, you know what I'm talking about.

Multiple yeast fermentations also play a part in creating improved flavor and texture. The chemistry is so cool!

If you ever try kneading dough by hand, you'll understand why the older bakers had Popeye arms. You're only working with a few pounds of dough. Try kneading fifty pounds of dough. We did this with rye bread one slow day at the bakery. We had a lot of fun throwing the dough around the table and punching it, but I couldn't imagine making dough without a mixer after that.

As gluten develops during kneading, you'll observe the changes that occur. The dough will go from a sticky, coarse mixture to a smooth elastic ball that will stretch without tearing. That's when you know it's ready.

I've done several experiments at home with bread, and I'm finding that dry yeast just doesn't have the staying power of fresh yeast. Therefore, I've added extra dry yeast to the final mix to pump a little extra dry yeast in the second stage. For some reason, I've only had this problem with bread. Fresh or cake yeast, in my opinion, makes a better loaf of bread.

When smashing air out of the dough, you can do this by simply pressing the air out on the table, but smacking the dough on the table was a good show for the customers and fun for the bakers. It was one of my favorite parts of the day.

You can thump the bottom of a loaf of bread after it's turned out to tell if it's done. If you thump it and it's not done, you'll get a deep, dull thud. If it's done, the sound is higher and hollow. If you've ever thumped a wall to find a stud, you'll know what I mean.

HOMEMADE WHITE BREAD

The Sponge

1 cup warm water
1 package dry active yeast or 2/3 oz. cake yeast
1½ cups all-purpose flour

Combine all ingredients and let rise until doubled. First fermentation.

The Bread

To the sponge add
½ cup milk
½ cup water
2 Tbs. sugar
2 tsp. salt
2 Tbs. + 1 tsp. shortening
½ pack dry yeast
3½ to 4 cups flour (we used all-purpose flour only; if you like crisper crusts, you can substitute some harder (high-gluten) bread flour —¼ bread flour to ¾ all purpose)

Combine all ingredients and knead in mixer, or by hand if so inclined.
Knead the dough 4 to 5 minutes if using a mixer, or about 15 to 20 minutes if by hand.
Place dough in a bowl that has been greased lightly so the dough won't stick.
Let the dough rise, covered, until at least double, approximately ½ to 1 hour.
Second fermentation.
Scale (measure) your dough into two portions: 1 lb. 3 oz. and 1 lb. 11 oz.
Round the dough into balls with your hands. Cover and let rise again in a warm area of room. Third fermentation.
Now we make the loaves.
With your hand, smash the air out of the dough ball and shape into a rectangle.
Using the now flattened rectangle of dough, starting at the top, fold the top ⅓ of the dough down, and with the heel of your hand seal it into the dough.
Fold down that combined piece over the remaining ⅓ and seal.

Finally, fold down and seal the side edges to form a loaf approximately the length of your bread pan. You may need to tuck the ends of your loaf back in before pressing them closed.

Place your loaf, seam side down, in a lightly oiled loaf pan. The smaller amount fits in an 8" x 4" pan; the larger piece fits a 9" x 5" pan.

Lightly coat the top of the loaf with just enough vegetable oil to cover the surface.

Covered, let rise in a warm area of room until loaf has doubled and filled out the corners of the pan. Fourth fermentation.

Preheat oven to 375 degrees.

Place pans in the center of upper rack and bake approximately 45 minutes until golden brown on top.

Dump the bread and let cool on a rack.

Yield: 2 loaves—one small (1 lb. 3 oz.) and one large (1 lb. 11 oz.)

BUTTERCRUST BREAD

This recipe is exactly the same as the homemade white with the following additional steps:

After proofing and just before putting the bread into the oven, cut the top of the loaf with five snips of the scissors and liberally wash the top with melted butter to suit your taste.

Bake as above for the homemade white.

After unmolding the bread, wash again with melted butter and let cool on a rack.

Yield: 2 loaves—one small, one large

WHOLE WHEAT BREAD

1 cup warm water
2 tsp. dry yeast
2 Tbs. honey
1 tsp. salt
1½ Tbs. shortening
2½ cups finely ground whole wheat flour

Mix all the ingredients, cover and let rise until doubled.

Shape into a loaf and place in small loaf pan.

Cover, put in a warm place and let rise until the pan is full.

Preheat oven to 375 degrees.

Bake approximately 45 minutes until golden brown on top.

Dump the bread and let cool on a rack.

Yield: 1 loaf

CINNAMON BREAD

For this recipe, you will need a 1-pound (16-oz.) piece of yellow dough (see page 109) for each loaf and between 1 to 1½ cups cinnamon smear per loaf (personal choice) (see page 140).

Roll the 1-pound piece of yellow dough into a rectangle about 15" tall and 9" wide. Brush the bottom edge with egg wash. Spread cinnamon smear on the remainder. Roll from the top (narrow end) down the length, letting the egg wash seal the loaf. Place in a *well-greased* Pullman loaf pan (what we called a sandwich mold).

Let the dough rise until the pan is almost full.

Preheat oven to 375 degrees.

Place pan in the center of upper rack and bake about one hour.

Test the loaf as you would for a cake, by pressing. When it rebounds, it's done.

Remove from oven and let rest in pan 10 minutes before removing.

Yield: 1 loaf

The more smear you use the richer it gets, but remember the dough can only support so much filling. As with all things, and especially in baking, "More is not always better."

At the bakery, we had real heavy metal three-strap molds that were used only for cinnamon bread. They were treated like schnecken molds and washed only in hot water so as to keep them seasoned. If you don't have a small Pullman pan, you can use a heavy glass loaf pan. A regular bread pan can be used, but keep an eye on the crust, as it may get quite dark before the inside is done.

As with all breads—and this is the hard part—you have to wait until it is cool enough to slice.

Toasted and buttered, this was certainly one of the most popular items, including with my daughter. I remember slicing the loaf when still warm because she wouldn't wait, spreading it with the already warm butter and watching her pull the center out and eat it first. The crust usually got left behind as she went for the next center.

When I was little, I remember my sisters pulling out the centers of the sweet rolls and cinnamon bread and giving me the crusts or outside piece. They loved me so much.

Cinnamon bread also makes excellent French toast and bread pudding.

HEARTH BREAD—FRENCH AND VIENNA

1 cup slightly warm water
2 tsp. dry yeast / 1 package
Bloom the yeast in water—about 5 minutes.

Add:
1 tsp. sugar
1¼ tsp. salt
1 tsp. shortening
2½ cups bread flour

Mix remaining ingredients and knead about 10 minutes to develop gluten.
Grease bowl, add dough, cover and let proof until doubled in size.
Punch dough.
Round into a ball, cover and let proof for about 15 minutes (sometimes called a bench rest).
Depending on what you're making, shape the dough—shorter loaves for Vienna bread or a longer loaf for French bread—and proof again.
After proofing, egg wash (half and half mixture with water) the top of the loaf.
Vienna was topped with sesame, poppy, cornmeal or just left plain.
Of course, no seeds on the French bread.
The bread is then scored with a sharp knife on the diagonal with about 2" between slits.
Preheat oven to 425 degrees.

For hearth breads, the lower the water temperature used above, the longer the fermentation. The longer the fermentation, the better the yeast develops. Don't go too cold, however, or you'll be waiting all day. I like my hearth bread to first ferment between one and two hours.

At the bakery, we would put the dough on boards with cornmeal and, after proofing, slide them into the oven. At home, you can use yellow cornmeal on a metal pan or simply use parchment paper on a pan.

For a crisper crust on hearth bread, you will need steam in your oven. Ours was steam injected, which made it easy. At home, you can place a pan on the bottom rack of the oven, let it get hot and add water just before you place your bread on the top rack. This will provide enough steam to give you a crisp crust.

If you're a fanatic about hearth bread, you can buy oven bricks or a pizza stone for your oven that will simulate a stone hearth. They are also a good investment for pizza. You will either need a wood bread peel covered with cornmeal or turn a sheet pan upside down. Then you can slide the bread off the peel or pan onto the oven bricks. This is as close as you'll get to a true hearth oven unless you have your own pizza oven in the backyard.

Put the bread in the center of upper rack. After 5 minutes, reduce heat to 375 degrees and bake until golden brown.

Yield: 1 loaf of Vienna bread or 1 loaf of French bread

Dinner Rolls

For many families, Virginia Bakery butter bits (also known as bread ends), knots, butter fans and brown-n-serve butter rolls played a significant role in every holiday and celebratory meal for as long as they can remember. For whatever reason, these families seldom considered including the yeast dinner rolls as an accompaniment to everyday meals. However, given an occasion for a formal dinner, the menu was not complete without warm, soft rolls fresh from the oven.

Tom Thie once said that when he thinks about yeast dinner rolls, Thanksgiving comes to mind because of the huge demand for them. "When the store opened on the Wednesday morning before Thanksgiving, all the cases would be stacked and the refrigerators and freezers would be packed. By early afternoon, not a single roll remained." Deborah Rieselman reported in her *Clifton Living* community newspaper article that right "before Thanksgiving, 400 packages of brown & serve rolls were sold, and customers were fighting over the last few dozen." According to Annie Glenn, certain customers got "angry with other customers for what they thought should be 'their Brown and Serve rolls' if there weren't enough to go around. It was nuts in there…and the lines to get in and the parking lot." On a more sentimental note, Sandra Thie Holzman shared that to this day people at her church, when having dinners, ask if she brought any of the Virginia Bakery rolls and "it can set me to tears."

For other folks, memories are more strongly attached to Christmas and Easter. On these holidays, as serving dishes were carried to the dining room,

The "secret" to making delicious dinner rolls is first in the use of real pieces of butter folded into the dough. Second is having several proofs, allowing the yeast plenty of time to create the delicious flavor. And last, mixing the dough until the elasticity is right, meaning that the dough has been mixed enough that it pulls away from the bowl but not over mixed and too hot. Armed with the following recipes, you're ready to give them a try!

one or two of the rolls disappearing before they reached the table was not uncommon. The culprits who split open the rolls right out of the warming oven and added a dab of creamy butter were no doubt easy to identify by the telltale licking of fingers as they sat down at the table. The smell of warm yeast rolls truly was enticing, and the slight sweetness along with the texture was just too tempting to resist. And so the understandable thievery was forgiven.

According to other stories, for special occasion morning brunches, the melt-in-your-mouth rolls added joy to the meals—whether they were topped with butter, honey and jams or prepared as very tasty sandwiches with ham, beef tenderloin or turkey.

WHITE ROLL DOUGH

This recipe is the basis for most of the dinner rolls.

7 tsp. instant yeast (2 Tbs. + 1 tsp.)
1 cup warm water
1 cup warm milk
1 egg
5 Tbs. sugar
2 tsp. salt
4 Tbs. shortening
4 Tbs. butter
6 cups all-purpose flour (or preferably 5 cups all-purpose flour and 1 cup bread or high-gluten flour)

Dissolve yeast in water and milk.

While yeast blooms, add all other ingredients.

Dough will be slightly loose but will tighten and form a ball as the mixer develops the gluten.

This usually takes about five to ten minutes, depending on the mixer. As the gluten develops, the dough will form a ball and pull away from the sides of the bowl. That's when you know it's ready.

Scrape down the bowl, remix dough and scrape again.

Oil the bowl using oil, a half oil–half butter mix or spray with pan spray.

Cover and let proof (first time) until doubled in size—about ½ hour to 1 hour.

Punch down in center, smashing the air out, and gather into a ball.

Yield: approximately 4 lbs.

BUTTER BITS / BREAD ENDS

Although there are people who swear these are different things, the butter bits and bread ends are the same. The confusion is based on what your grandma called them.

This recipe uses one pound (16 oz.) of white roll dough (see page 211).

Make the rolls by taking the one-pound piece of dough and, on a floured surface, roll the dough into a rectangle approximately 9" x 12". Split 2 ounces (½ stick) of butter (cool but close to room temperature is easiest to work with) into 16 pieces and place on bottom ⅔ of dough as shown in Diagram #1:
(A) Fold top ⅓ of dough over the eight pieces of butter in the center.
(B) Fold the bottom ⅓ with the remaining butter up and over this.

Diagram #2:
Turn dough a quarter turn.
Diagram #3:
(A) Fold the top third down over the center.
(B) Fold the bottom third up and over that. This is called a tri-fold.

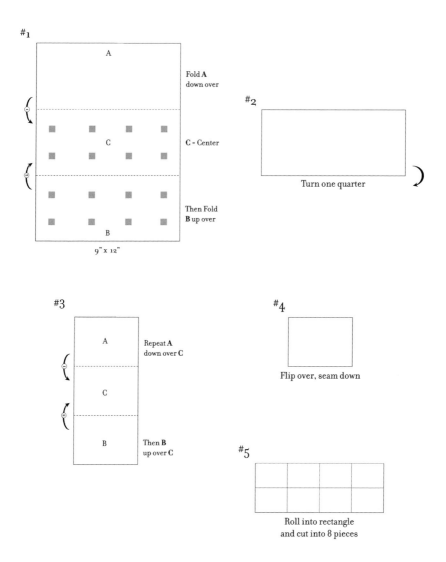

Diagram #4:
Turn this piece over and let rest in refrigerator on a floured plate covered with a cloth for ½ hour. This step keeps the butter cold.
Diagram #5:
Roll dough into 5" x 8" rectangle.
Cut into eight equal size pieces and place them on a greased baking pan.
Proof, covered, until doubled.
Preheat oven to 375 degrees.

Place pan in the center of upper rack and bake approximately 20 minutes until golden brown on top.
Remove rolls from pan and let cool on a rack.

Yield: 8 rolls

BROWN-N-SERVE ROLLS

To make brown-n-serve rolls, follow the recipe for butter bits through the third proofing, when the rolls have doubled in size.

Preheat oven to 350 degrees.
Put the brown-n-serve pieces in the oven and turn off the heat. Let them bake for 7 to 10 minutes. Ideally, the yeast should be cooked and the dough set, but the roll should not brown. If the dough is not done enough, the dough will collapse and you'll have a greasy mess. Again, you can use the touch test. The dough will spring back when it's ready. Better to err on the side of too brown than underdone.
Remove from oven and allow to cool completely before wrapping and storing. These rolls can be stored for 3 to 4 days in the refrigerator, 2 to 3 months in the freezer.
When you are ready to use the rolls, allow them to reach room temperature and bake at 375 degrees for approximately 10 minutes, until golden brown.

> Many people preferred the brown-n-serve because of that final onsite baking. I'm sure there are a lot of memories there. The smell, sight and taste.

BUTTER FANS

The recipe uses one pound (16 oz.) of white roll dough (see page 211).
Follow directions for butter bits (see page 212) through the steps shown in Diagram #5, ending up with a 5" x 8" rectangle.
Roll the dough again and give it one more tri-fold, creating a smaller rectangle. Keep the dough about 1" thick.

Dinner Rolls

This is my favorite dinner roll.

Cut the dough into 8 small squares and turn them on their sides as you place them into a greased muffin mold. You should see the layers of butter and dough.

Proof, covered, until doubled.

Preheat oven to 375 degrees.

Place pan in the center of upper rack and bake approximately 20 minutes until golden brown on top.

Remove rolls from pan and let cool on a rack.

Yield: 8 rolls

Knots

This recipe uses one pound (16 oz.) of white roll dough (see page 211).

Using the one-pound piece of dough, roll pieces the size you want—about a golf ball size is fine.

Roll the balls into sticks about 5" long and then tie each stick in a single knot.

If you want to get fancy, you can roll the stick longer and make a double knot.

Place the knotted dough on a greased or parchment-lined pan.

Proof, covered, until doubled.

Brush with egg wash (equal amounts of whole egg and water) and add sesame seeds, poppy seeds or both. Plain knots can be washed with egg mixture or a melted butter wash.

Preheat oven to 375 degrees.

Place pan in the center of upper rack and bake approximately 15 to 20 minutes until done. You're looking for a nice golden brown. When you touch the roll, it should spring back. If it leaves a dent, it's "knot" quite done. Remove rolls from pan and let cool on a rack.

Yield: 8 rolls

HARD ROLLS

Hard rolls use the same dough as the hearth breads. Follow the directions given for making the French and Vienna bread dough (see page 208).

Punch dough and portion dough into small pieces.
Round into balls, cover and let proof for about 15 minutes (sometimes called a bench rest).
Shape the dough into "miniature loaves of bread."

Place them on a parchment-lined baking sheet and proof again.
After proofing, apply egg wash (mixture of equal parts whole egg and water) to the tops of the rolls, and then slice the tops once.
Cover the tops with sesame seeds or poppy seeds, or just leave them plain.
Preheat oven to 425 degrees.
Put the rolls in the oven in the center of the upper rack. After 5 minutes, reduce heat to 375 degrees and bake approximately 15 minutes until golden brown.

You can make hard rolls any size you want. At the bakery, we would use a piece of dough about the size of a golf ball.

Yield: approximately a dozen to 16 rolls

Virginia Bakery Employees

While we have tried our best to list all the people who worked at Virginia Bakery over the years, we may have missed some folks or been unable to discover their first or last names. We apologize in advance if we did not include someone who should have been on this list.

BAKERS, PORTERS, ASSISTANTS AND GOFERS

Jerry Armstead
Ed Arnult
Joe "JD" Arnult
George Ashford
Donald Baskins
Tim Beckmeyer
Tom Beischel
Charlie Bell
Roger "Big Rog" Byrd
Royce "Roy" Byrd
Andy Corbett
Tim "Dusty" Couch
Slim Daniels
Roosevelt "Rosie" Davis

Will Dawson
Carl "Juice" De Armond
Lou Dorsey
"Dumby" _____
Dwayne "Gip" Gibson
Jeff Grisom
Charlie Hensey
Chris Huff
_____ Huffelmeier
Hermie Lee Jackson
George Jones
Tony "Bird" Jones
John Kelley
Jim Lawrence

Virginia Bakery Employees

Willie Little
Dillon Lockwood
Joe Mussburger
August "Gus" Nolte
Fred "Fritz" Pieper
Bill Pritz
_____ Reichers
Gary Roberson
Joe Roth
Berthold Schwegmann
Wilbur Smith

"Red" Louis Suhre
Dick Thie
James "Jimmy" Thie
Mark Thie
Paul Thie Jr.
"Price Hill Bill" Thie
Jim Turner
Dusty Umbach
Frank Weber
Wayne Williams
Jim Wilson

Shop Girls and Decorators

Helen Adams
Megan Archdeacon
Elizabeth Barber
Emily Barber
Julie Beckmeyer
Nicole Belmont
Esther Billman
Connie Cawthorne
Katie Cawthorne
Wendy Cawthorne
Jennifer Counts
Veronica De Armond
Emma _____
Virginia Hasslinger Gardner
Sarah Wander Geis
Lyda Giddeon
Annie Glenn
Martha Greek
Melinda Greek
Stephanie Hall
Veronica Holland
Chris Huff
Jewel _____
Emily Kaderli
Stella Kaiser
Kristine Kessler
Laurie Lehrter
Courtney Lockwood

Meredith Lockwood
Maria _____
Marie_____
Myrna Thie Matthew
Marion Ranz Maujer
Sophie McManus
Eula Montgomery
Gert Moore
Theresa Nacke
Ionna Paraskevepoulos
Beth Ranker
Kim Ranker
Elaine Richardson
Cora Samad
Anne Schreiber
Patty Schroeck
Charlotte Siegler
Ruth Sheppard
Amanda Slater
Karen Streit
Lydia Thie
Barbara Weishaar
Stephanie Weithofer-Hicks
Christine Wilfinger
Kathy Willams
Marian Wullenweber
Michelle Zobay

List of Contributors

Eunie Abel's wedding cake came from Virginia Bakery, which was *the* reputed place to purchase wedding cakes, as did her mother's wedding cake in 1936. The top groom's cake was chocolate and was kept in the freezer for a year, awaiting their first anniversary. Beyond the icing, the cake was topped with a china basket of live flowers. She was sorry when the bakery closed and she had to look elsewhere for her daughter's wedding cake.

Mary Anne Acree, secretary for the Greater Cincinnati Retail Bakers Association, was introduced to Virginia Bakery's cinnamon coffee cake when she was a little girl. She married "Sonny," a baker who joined GCRBA, met Bill Thie and enjoyed the annual picnics. After she and Sonny joined the Young Bakers, they met Howard and Cindy, two of the finest people she has ever known. She remembers Howard's raspberries, which he picked and used at the bakery.

Helen Adams holds Virginia Bakery in a special place of her heart. She grew up across the street from Moe Thie, got her first real job at the bakery working behind the counter during the holiday season and feels that her experience in the store taught her many invaluable lessons. Her favorite treat was always the chocolate cake with white icing, but she also loved schnecken.

Jan Leader Ahern loved the Virginia Bakery! She is the granddaughter of Mrs. Biechler and grew up on Loraine, in Clifton, near the bakery. She spent many hours shopping for her grandmother. The best "free" cookies were the thin, crispy sugar and the swirled butter cookies. She has *never* found comparable recipes for those cookies. Her other favorites were gems and leaf loaf. She looks forward to *finally* finding out how to make these recipes.

Marjorie Allen was introduced to the Virginia Bakery by Dorothy Stolzenbach Payne, her daughter Stephanie's piano teacher who lived in Clifton. On recital days, Mrs. Payne always served sugarcoated doughnuts that melted in your mouth! It became a habit to shop there while Stephanie was in her lesson to pick up doughnuts, pastries, birthday cakes, etc. to take home to Glendale. Such great memories.

Growing up in a house on the corner of Brookline and Hosea, it was a given that **Janet Fast Andress** was an aficionado of Virginia Bakery goodies. She would often walk to the bakery with her grandmother, Amelia Eberle, who knew the owner. Janet enjoyed being with her grandmother and, secondly, she liked always receiving a warm cookie from Mrs. Thie. It is no wonder she has pleasant memories of Virginia Bakery—more than seventy years later!

Jerry Armstead worked at Virginia Bakery for ten years. During that time he "did it all"—watched the ovens, made all types of dough, delivered wedding cakes and interacted with customers, especially the early people who came to the back door for doughnuts because they "needed it bad." One time he even took part in a commercial for CG&E in which they filmed his hands making bread. "Working at Virginia Bakery made you versatile."

Edward "Eddie" Arnult started working at Virginia Bakery in 1945 at the age of fourteen. Bill ("The Boss") hired him for a wide variety of duties that grew as he did, including the beer runs and preparing pans for the next day's baking use. He worked after school and on Saturdays (starting at 7:00 a.m. and finishing around 5:00 p.m.). Hard work with laughter. High-quality bakery goods. Great people!

Nancy Sahnd Bauman was raised on Virginia Bakery bread and never had the other stuff until she was on her own. Her family can still taste and visualize the cinnamon coffee cake, the butter cake, the coconut white cake, the cookies and so on. Virginia Bakery made her wedding cake and her sister's. The shop was a big part of their lives, and they still have trouble imagining Clifton without Virginia Bakery.

Merritt Beischel started going to Virginia Bakery when in utero and continued to do so until they closed the doors.

Cooking has always been a joy for **Rosemary Beischel**, especially trying new recipes. As her children became teenagers, she found more time to experiment with yeast breads and coffee cake recipes. She never tires of reading cookbooks; so when Cynthia asked her if she would test some of the recipes from Virginia Bakery that would appear in her and Tom Thie's book, she was delighted.

Tom Beischel was a classmate all through high school and a dear friend of Howard Thie ever after. As a student from 1942 to 1944, he worked only on Saturdays (from 4:00 a.m. to 4:00 p.m.) doing nothing but the simplest of tasks, mainly in the basement: preparing pans, washing equipment, filling doughnuts, powdering sweet rolls, etc. Now a priest, he presided over Howard's funeral in 1999. He thanks the Thie family.

Jim Bender has many fond memories of growing up in Clifton, and of course, the Virginia Bakery was part of that experience in a large way. He remembers the wonderful smells, seeing Tom's dad pull hot baked bread from the rotating oven and watching the ladies slice the bread. "It was a sad day when customers were no longer able to buy their baked goods."

Marilyn Bixler fondly recollects going to the Virginia Bakery as wonderful. The relationship lasted almost sixty years. She grew up eating yummy things from there, but the most wonderful was the schnecken. Just hearing the word makes her mouth water. She attributes her childhood chubbiness, in part, to the bakery. Going to the bakery every Saturday morning was the highlight of her week growing up and continued to be so after she moved from Clifton.

Angelita Bondoc has excellent memories of Virginia Bakery. She was a customer "way, way back," shopping there three times a week. Their service was excellent, and by her own admission, she was particular—she liked things light and gooey. Her favorite was definitely schnecken, but she also liked the breads, butterscotch gems, pecan pie and Mexican wedding cookies. It was a wonderful place to get bakery goods. Everything was in "A" shape in Virginia Bakery.

Laurie Bredenfoerder had the good fortune to work at Good Samaritan Hospital, within walking distance of the Virginia Bakery, for most of her early professional life. The cake-less, all-icing birthday "cake" that Laurie special-ordered for her mother is only one of the unique, delicious memories that Virginia Bakery created for her.

Wes Carney's good friend Kristine Kessler worked at Virginia Bakery decorating wedding cakes for many years, and she introduced him to her co-worker, Stephanie Hall, who was working her way through college. Wes used to go and hang out and talk with them while they were working there during the early and mid-1990s. To give the Cliff Notes version, he later married Stephanie. And Virginia Bakery made their wedding cake.

In childhood, **Mark G. Carroll** began accompanying his parents to Virginia Bakery, where they bought all of their bread and other products, and Grandma Thie would give him cookies. One winter, during a family visit, Mark made a cup of tea for Hattie. Apparently, he made quite an impression—after that, she would always give him a bag of cookies. Years later, training as a general surgeon at Good Samaritan Hospital, he shopped there often.

Barbara Clark's grandfather (George W. Felss of the Felss Flour Milling Co.) sold flour, sugar and shortening to the Virginia Bakery. Her parents had their wedding cake (1952) and fiftieth-anniversary cake (2002) made at the Virginia Bakery. She remembers her grandmother always bought buttercrust bread and the round German cheesecake from the bakery.

When **Jane Corlett Zachman** and **Glen Corlett** were children growing up in Westwood, their special treat was a trip to Clifton and the Virginia Bakery. Their favorite pastries were the filled Danish rolls and the special Virginia Bakery cheesecake. It must have been a secret recipe, because they have never tasted a cheesecake that was as delicious.

Alice Derrick remembers how the Annunciation School staff "lived for Virginia reels on Thursday. You would have to get there early before they were gone. Nothing hurt like getting there too late, except knowing they are closed. There will never be another bakery like that." Her husband has the special memory of his grandmother walking him to Virginia Bakery as a small child fifty years ago, treating him to the start of a great day.

Dennis Doggett is a maternal nephew of the Thies. His relationship with Virginia Bakery was through the family with "tasty" exposures to the Virginia Bakery goods at holiday celebrations, as well as summer visits as a child with the Thies, where he stayed with his cousin sharing good times and good food. He also remembers the wonderful aromas and visual eye candy behind the glass display cases. A place to die for!

Mildred Doggett, the older sister, confidante and lifelong friend of Cindy Thie, offered stories and photos for this book. Unfortunately, Mildred died on October 19, 2009, at the age of eighty-four, before she could provide further information, but her old news clippings were seen by her son Dennis and forwarded.

Barbara Peterson Donovan was introduced to Virginia Bakery through grandmothers who lived in Clifton. She has vivid memories of the cookies and the wonderful, buttery aroma of the bakery.

Theresa Fisher remembers having little gems every Christmas brunch. Her mom, Barb Leugers, was a loyal customer and ordered more schnecken than anyone when the bakery closed its full-service retail shop.

Orene Copelan Foreman grew up in Clifton, graduated from UC and married at Calvary Church. Her bakery was always Virginia Bakery. Mrs. Thie used to give cookies to her and her brother. Her dad used to say, "If only I could be turned loose in Virginia Bakery with a pot of hot coffee!" Her four children were raised on their bread, rolls and schnecken. Three daughters had wedding cakes from there. She'll always remember those "Golden Days."

Evie and David Foulkes took lots of walks with their son Chris when he was a crying newborn. Every Saturday morning, they would walk down Clifton Avenue and be at the Virginia Bakery door at 6:00 a.m. Schnecken was the highlight of the day! Their pediatrician said he saw them every Saturday morning when he drove to the hospital and asked, "Where do you go at that hour of the morning?" Thank goodness for Virginia Bakery!

Judy Trombly Ganance lived a four-minute walk away from the bakery. She didn't have a personal relationship with any of the staff, but she sees them in her visual memory like it was yesterday! On her eighth birthday, the cake that came from Virginia Bakery had big, gorgeous yellow icing roses that completely upstaged any other part of the cake. Yellow was the color of happiness on that special day.

Joyzell Friason George grew up in Mount Auburn along with her parents and four brothers. Little did she know how much Virginia Bakery would affect her life and her unborn son, Robert Mynatt. She remembers escapades of going to get "sweets" with her grandmother, Vivian Shrout; father, A. Vernon Friason; and friend, Sheila Burney Douglas. Running into people later in life who also enjoyed Virginia Bakery shows how a "little" bakery affected a whole lot of people.

Annie Marie Glenn was a Clifton resident and worked at Virginia Bakery for six years, during which time she was a store clerk, cookie decorator and helped with taking care of Carly Thie. She received a bachelor of arts in communication from the University of Cincinnati. She currently lives in Scottsdale, Arizona, where she enjoys volunteering, writing, photography, yoga and baking.

Denise "Denny" Mohan Grawe grew up in Clifton. The Virginia Bakery was a weekly part of her family's life. She loved going there with her mom, Jane Mohan, who always bought the family's favorite pastries and cakes, as each family member had their personal preferences. Denny's mother liked to boast that her husband, Dr. John Mohan, delivered the Thie children, thus making their bond with Virginia Bakery even more personal.

Zachary Green grew up in the Gaslight District of Clifton. As a kid, he enjoyed looking at the mirror display by the ceiling of all the birthday cakes. As a teenager, he worked next door at Skyline as a busboy/dishwasher and always saw the flour-stained sidewalk and stoop leading up to the bakery's back door—which was black and yellow—showing the decades of dry goods that had been embedded into those areas.

Bill Hartman, owner of the St. Lawrence Bakery, belonged to the community of Cincinnati bakers. When he first started out, Bill Thie gave him some advice; later, he and Howard Thie started the Young Bakers Club. He remembers coming into Virginia Bakery and eating some of their items—he liked the Danish coffee cakes.

Janet Hengstenberg Hauck remembers going to Virginia Bakery with her mother who, appropriately for the time, wore a dress hat and white gloves when going shopping. At that time, bread was ten cents a loaf. "Trips to the bakery as a child were wonderful occasions—lots of fun. There's never been a bakery like it."

Marjorie Heim's grandmother lived on Hosea, and she used to shop for her every Saturday. Of course, she had to stop at Virginia Bakery to pick up what she needed, which was always a filled tea ring and a cinnamon crumb cake, and maybe some gems. Years later, she had a house built on Jessup Road that turned out to be right across the street from Janet Thie.

Kristine Kessler Hess worked at Virginia Bakery for seven years. She started in the summer of 1988 as a store clerk/cashier and worked her way up to decorating cookies and, soon after, cakes. The Thie family was like a second family to her during those years: Howard and Tom taught her how to cook, and Virginia and Maureen taught her how to decorate cakes, including wedding cakes.

Carol Heutcher's uncle, Fred "Fritz" Pieper, was a longtime employee at Virginia Bakery. Both her uncle and his wife, Esther, were friends of Bill and Myrtle Thie. She knows the bakers worked very hard and produced excellent baked goods that were known all over the city.

Born and raised in Cincinnati of Irish/German parents, **Debbi Lysaght Hill**'s love of bread comes quite naturally. Diagnosed with thyroid cancer at thirty-nine, the news got even worse when treatments involved a long diet of no iodine, a key ingredient in almost everything, including bread. The doctor sent her to Virginia Bakery. One piece of their specially made bread a day was her prize for enduring another day of treatment. She still remembers the taste.

Leigh Ismael did not always live close to Virginia Bakery, but her family always made sure they had a cherry-topped coffee cake for their Christmas brunch.

Paul Jaeger was the owner of Jaeger's Clifton Meat Market, which was on Ludlow Avenue. Paul's son Donald made sure his family purchased some of the five strap pans used for making schnecken when Virginia Bakery's equipment was auctioned on January 12, 2006. In July 2009, those pans became a beanbag toss game for the grandchildren at the Jaeger Schnecken Fest Family Reunion.

Jan Jauch, **Robert Samad**, **Sandy Schneeman**, **Mary Ann Lohmueller** and **Tricia Conrad** were about ages eight to thirteen when they heard Grandma "Cora" Samad talk about Virginia Bakery, but they all remember how much she enjoyed working there. It was her life after her husband passed away and gave her the energy and will to live. When they all think about their father's mother, they always think of her in her white apron and Virginia Bakery.

Mary Judge lived in Clifton for a number of years and was a true schnecken fan. Working as the orchestra librarian at Music Hall, she knew Erich Kunzel, who was also very fond of schnecken. When the store announced it was closing, she sent him a message with the subject title "never to be again." His response was, "Buy up everything you can!"

Beth Kautzman remembers being pushed in a stroller for frequent trips to Virginia Bakery as a young child. Later in life, she remembers being a member of the Schnecken Club. Both she and her mother had Virginia Bakery make their wedding cakes.

Jane Arnult Knueven passed the bakery at least two times a day going to and from school, and she remembers the delicious smells that surrounded the building. Her fond memories of Virginia Bakery include delicious foods such as filled tea rings, double butter coffee cakes and then there was her birthday cake!

Earl Kramer was the owner of the Cincinnati Bakers' Supply Company and had the privilege of knowing Bill, Myrtle, Howard and Cindy. He remembers Virginia Bakery as being "a great bakery and a very good pay."

Tim Lanham remembers schnecken as the most glorious sticky bun with a full layer of sticky goodness on top. In addition to Virginia Bakery's special breads and famous wedding cakes, he also remembers another of his favorites, Virginia reel doughnuts. He hasn't found anyone that makes them as good since or, for that matter, makes them at all. One of their doughnuts and a cold glass of milk, and all was right with the world.

Marilyn Leathers remembers her first introduction to schnecken. She was hooked. From then on, family and friends received gifts of the fantastic, tasty delight for Christmas, birthdays or "just because." She kept a frozen supply on hand so that when company came, they could count on this treat, and she usually sent them home with a package of schnecken too.

Mark Leathers often stayed with his Aunt Cindy and Uncle Howard (Thie) after family gatherings. One time, he, his cousin Tom and his brother Tom were at the bakery while Howard finished his work. They were allowed to choose whatever their hearts were set on, and the phrase "kid in a candy store" was fulfilled that day. Fortunately for them, they were not allowed to consume all the chosen items in their entirety at once!

Barb Leugers had Moe Thie laughing when Virginia Bakery was in its final days of regular operation because of how many schnecken she was buying. Even before the closing, she was known to buy six or more at a time. She taught this love to her son, who became known as the Schnecken King of Denver, thanks to her shipping them out to Colorado.

Connie Schawann Lindsay grew up on Virginia Bakery baked goods. Her dad would always buy her, her brother and her sister a cream horn… along with other delicious items. When she married, she got her husband, **Scott**, hooked on Virginia Bakery as well. Her family members would all take turns "running" to the bakery for one another. They have yet to find a bakery that comes close to having the delicious breads and sweet goods they enjoyed at Virginia Bakery.

Ruth Wessel Lipps, at age ninety, has fond memories of Virginia Bakery at Clifton and Ludlow Avenues. Whenever she was in Clifton, she would stop at the bakery. They always had something good, including biscuits, cookies and coffee cakes, but most of all the schnecken at holiday times. She and her family do miss the bakery.

Dorothy Long, sister of Cindy Thie, thoroughly enjoyed all the German-influenced baked goods that Virginia Bakery made, but especially the almond croissant cookies and the rolls. Dorothy remembers how the family would get together for all the birthdays and holidays and how Cindy decorated a cake for their brother Tom's fiftieth birthday with fifty candles (which he was unable to blow out, even with lots of huffing and puffing).

Beth Luessen and her husband **Wayne** were married on November 25, 1983, and they got their wedding cake, a delicious carrot cake, from Virginia Bakery! They've continued to have carrot cake every year on their anniversary, and they got them from Virginia Bakery as long as the store was open. Unfortunately, they've had to switch to another bakery.

Brian Messmore was first introduced to Virginia Bakery, its baked goods and the special people working there when he was working as an EMT for Shoemaker Ambulance. He has fond memories of the place and remembers good pastries!

Virginia Bakery provided **Lindsay Beischel Miklos** and her family with many tasty moments, including late-night coffee cake snacks over the kitchen island, butter bits and butterscotch gems on Christmas morning and smiley face cookies that were finished before they even left the parking lot.

Jane Mohan recalls accompanying her mom on innumerable shopping trips that began with Keller's Grocery and almost always ended with Virginia Bakery. If it wasn't on the agenda, she discovered that a mix of begging and whining generally did the trick. That cookie that one of the bakery's employees would "surreptitiously" slip her was a necessity, and the warm, freshly sliced loaves of bread that rarely made it home…well, they were worth any scolding.

When **Kevin Mohan** was young, he'd go to Virginia Bakery at least weekly with his mother. She would buy fresh bread, doughnuts, crumb cake or sometimes a cake for a special occasion. The bakery smelled great and was busy with customers. The ladies working behind the counter would always give him a free cookie as they waited. Virginia Bakery had the best darn cookies and crumb cake of any bakery that he's ever visited.

A native of Knoxville, Tennessee, **Ibbie L. Muntz** lived and raised her children in Cincinnati from 1976 to 1983 and then back again in 1984–85 and from 2005 to 2008. Her husband, **John Muntz**, a Cincinnati native and an avid Bearcat fan, loved childhood visits to Virginia Bakery with his mother, especially the ones to purchase a cookie after a trip to the dentist across Clifton Avenue. Virginia Bakery nourished their families for at least three generations!

Amy Nadicksbernd has very fond memories of her grandfather coming to her family's house and bringing them enormous yummy éclairs, and that was a very special treat.

Susan W. Newmark worked at the Hebrew Union College in the 1980s. It wasn't long before she discovered the Virginia Bakery down the street. Over the years, she especially loved the tea cookies. She learned which day they were baked and rarely missed buying a selection on this day and others! Long after moving on professionally, she still stopped by for the moist bran muffins and tea cookies—among other treats.

Dick Nichols, who ran C&L Motors in the 1940s with Neil Pheipher, has wonderful memories of Virginia Bakery. Their used car lot was next door to the bakery, and they built a log cabin for their office. He remembers how many times customers would get a number from the bakery, go across the street to the grocery store and come back to the bakery to purchase their baked goods—all before their number was called.

Daniel Peterson's strongest memory, other than the good-tasting bakery products, was the interior of the store in the 1950s and the blue-tinted mirror.

Diana Porter, a friend of Jennifer Thie, has lived within five miles of the Virginia Bakery for the last forty years. She took every opportunity she could to stop by, and Mr. Thie often came out to say hello. While she loved the schnecken, the carrot cake was her favorite.

Bill Pritz, owner of Shadeau Breads, had his first bakery job at Virginia Bakery, where he realized there was something there that interested him. That job became the inspiration for his decision to pursue baking as a career and provided a standard to follow and emulate.

Judy Reinhold has fond memories of visits to Virginia Bakery, including being late for or missing UC classes to buy a special treat. During the 1978 blizzard, while school was closed, she made the trek to pick up her grandpa's birthday cake. Her car, with frozen doors kept closed with her scarf, went off the road. With a friendly push back onto the street, she was home in time for the family gathering—cake in hand.

Bill Rembold and his wife, Nancy, met Janet, Howard's sister, at Monfort Heights Methodist Church. Their son, Scotty, had cerebral palsy, and Janet's daughters, Martha and Melinda, along with Howard's daughters, Jennifer and Deborah, helped with Scotty's home therapy program. Bill also helped Howard on occasion when he was shorthanded and needed someone to deliver wedding cakes.

Mary Rinsky is a retired psychologist who has a sweet tooth. Her family went to Virginia Bakery once a week when she was a little girl in the 1950s. She always wanted to get the ticket from the ticket machine, and she clearly remembers the ladies handing her a butter cookie treat. She adored their angel food cakes; they had a smooth, fluffy, moist texture that she's never had in another angel food.

Mel Rueger used to accompany his friends, Harry Guten, Dan Teehan, and Ray Shannon, to Virginia Bakery as young professionals in the 1960s. The foursome enjoyed getting behind the counters and "helping" to sell things. He enjoyed their specialty, Schnecken.

A Pittsburgh native, **Tim Ruffner** has lived in Cincinnati since 1998. One February day in 1999 while walking from Corryville to the Ludlow Avenue Skyline, Tim stopped in the Virginia Bakery to inquire about the "Apartment for Rent" sign in the front window. Over the next five years, the Virginia Bakery, its people and its products became a memorable and meaningful part of his life and home at 288 Ludlow Avenue.

Cherie Lynn Nolte Sauer's memories of Virginia Bakery go back to the 1940s growing up on "day-old" treats that her Grandpa (Gus) Nolte sent home. Her wedding cake also came from Virginia Bakery as a gift from her grandfather. The cake was an unusual chapel style, and there were figures of the entire wedding party—with the ladies in colors of the attendants' dresses—and the minister.

Nancy Sauerbeck's mother, Marian Wullenweber, was a longtime employee of Virginia Bakery who made lifelong friends with her customers and co-workers. Nancy remembers her getting up at 2:30 a.m. to go pack Christmas cookies. Every Saturday, she brought home the "bakery rags" to soak and wash for Monday morning and often had home orders to deliver around the neighborhood. Nancy and her siblings particularly enjoyed their special wedding cakes from Virginia Bakery.

Robert J. and **Ruth Schawann** and family of Hamilton, Ohio, started coming to Virginia Bakery in the 1950s when sales trips would take Bob to downtown Cincinnati. After he retired, Bob and Ruth would make a trip down every couple of months to stock up on baked goods. They got to know the staff very well. They were very sad when the bakery closed.

Helen Schwegmann's husband, Bert, was a baker at Virginia Bakery for many years before he left to open his own bakery. She knew Hattie Thie, as well as Bill and Myrtle, and she and her husband became friends with the family, being invited to weddings and other social gatherings. Hattie knitted a sweater for her first baby. The rye bread was something she liked, as well as the brandy bump cookies at Christmastime.

Caroline Vogel Seim's memories go deeper than just the wonderful coffee cakes, cookies, breads and pastries. Her father, Lou Dorsey, was a baker for Virginia Bakery for over fifty years. On Friday evenings he worked by himself, getting things baked for Saturday mornings when the bakery opened. Sometimes Caroline would stop by and dip into a large tub of cinnamon crumbs he had made to top the cinnamon coffee cakes and rolls. Pure heaven!

Ellen Sibert is the daughter of Bert Schwegmann, a man who emigrated from Germany in the hopes of opening his own bakery one day. Over fifty years ago, Bill Thie gave him a chance to learn and work alongside Paul and Carl at the Virginia Bakery. That was the beginning of a great relationship. Although her father has been gone a long time, the stories of Virginia Bakery live on in her heart.

Dennis Smith's father, Omer, is the person who handmade white-lined corrugated cake circles for Bill Thie before they were a readily available product. He did this by pasting white shelf paper onto brown corrugated paper using his mother's flour and water for glue and cutting the circles out with a jig and used razor blades from a barbershop. The Paper Products Company still serves the baking industry. Virginia Bakery gave Omer the idea!

Chuck Snavely moved to Cincinnati in 1970 to join the CSO. He thinks that Cynthia was the one who led him down the high calorie path to schnecken nirvana at the Virginia Bakery. Chuck was hooked from the first bite and has since found some fellow travelers. One couple moved from Cincinnati to

New York City. He sent or took Virginia Bakery schnecken to them on more than one occasion, per request.

Joyce Steele lived in Clifton when first married and became very familiar with Virginia Bakery. Not liking to bake herself, she always knew she could get a nice assortment at the bakery by just pointing at the cases. She always bought her Christmas cookies there, even after they moved. She loved their bread, too, and having it sliced fresh from the oven. Her son, David, was in the Boy Scouts with Tom Thie.

Bill Sterwerf remembers Virginia Bakery playing a big part of his family's life when growing up. "Good Old Mr. (Lou) Dorsey," one of the bakers, lived next door and would bring home Bill's mother's bread order twice a week. The family's seven children enjoyed watching her deal out the bread slices as if they were a deck of playing cards. On weekends, their order would include a tea ring and a cinnamon crumb cake.

Karen Lockard Striet worked at Virginia Bakery as a teenager from 1962 to 1966. Her jobs included taking and packing items in the order department on Saturdays, packing the cookie case (and eating some of the broken ones), working the cash register and helping to decorate the window display that faced out by the left side door. The bakery was a fun place to work. The Thies were very nice people.

The eldest of seven children, **Kristina Chase Strom**'s family lived in Cincinnati for twelve years. Whenever her mom had a baby at Deaconess Hospital in Clifton, her dad would stop in at Virginia Bakery and buy a pecan Danish for himself and a bag of goodies to bring home. Even today, reminiscing about Cincinnati, her eighty-nine-year-old father says, "And I got to go to Virginia Bakery five times! Best Danish I ever tasted…"

Sally Strunk remembers family members and friends going to Virginia Bakery on a regular basis. Her mother-in-law's favorite item was the tea ring coffee cake. Sally's neighbor, Bob Driehaus, would go every Saturday and get schnecken for his family. Carolyn Hunter, her cousin, remembers that their Aunt Adele liked the good bread. Sally and Peter's wedding cake came from Virginia Bakery.

Jim Tallman used to go to the Virginia Bakery all the time, as he lived for a while in the apartment building on Howell directly opposite Keller's lower parking lot. He remembers the box with the red trademark and the red-and-white string that used to be tied around it. He and his friends used to get a really good raspberry Danish item, and he was very disappointed when they went out of business.

Carolyn Kuhn Taylor grew up in Clifton and was lucky enough to eat Virginia Bakery products weekly. Her grandfather, William Kuhn, supplied lard to the bakery. She got to know the bakers well because she worked around the corner. They once helped her when she locked herself out of the office. Her college sorority obtained large empty egg cans, creatively covered them and sold them as wastebaskets. Her first wedding cake came from Virginia Bakery.

Kristene (Templeton) Horn and **Julie Templeton** grew up eating Virginia Bakery's buttercrust bread out of the bag in the back of their mom's car. Their family still hasn't been able to find another bakery that can replicate the old recipes, and they dearly miss having Virginia Bakery on Ludlow. They live in Clifton.

Chris Trombly-Christen loved when her mother would ask her to run an errand to Virginia Bakery. With a dollar bill tightly held in her hand, she'd cut through the parking lot and get a whiff of whatever baked goods were being made. She enjoyed watching the bakers and counter ladies (with beehive hairdos) work, observing the cake figurines on display and especially receiving the free cookie, which she ate slowly all the way back home.

Thomas Wagner had friends who worked in Virginia Bakery's back shop in the 1940s and often entered the building through the back door. He remembers quality baked goods, as well as a fun crew. One of his memories is about ongoing games between Bill and Everist Ciccullo, the man who ran the Mobil Oil Station—including Bill throwing some dough balls across the street and then jumping behind the door so as not to be seen!

Jane Hess Walker has never had angel food cake like the ones made at Virginia Bakery. What she thinks made them special was the icing with the cakes. They almost tasted like vanilla sundaes. She's thought about trying to bake one, but she hasn't. Instead, when out, she thinks, "Oh, maybe that will taste like the one I remember from Virginia Bakery many years ago," buys one and when she gets it home…"Nah."

Warren Webster first became aware of "the place" while he was in medical school. He was working a part-time job in addition to going to school, and his wife, **Karen**, was also working at Children's Hospital. They had two children then and didn't have much time for leisure or socializing, but as members of the Schnecken Club they did treat themselves occasionally to a schnecken, which they had no problem consuming in one sitting.

Barb Weishaar worked at Virginia Bakery starting when she was in the eighth grade at Clifton school. Sandra Thie was in her class and got her the job. Barb bought her first two-wheel bike with her earnings. A picture was taken of Barb at the bakery for an advertisement in her Hughes High School yearbook. "The Virginia Bakery was the best ever; none in the city can come close to any of their baked goods."

Susan Sahnd Wood grew up in Clifton, and her family owned the Baiter and Sahnd Funeral Home near Virginia Bakery. Her father was friends with the Thies, so he went in the back door of the bakery every Friday afternoon and took home a huge bag of bakery products. Because her dad was a funeral director/embalmer, the bakers decided to play a joke on him: one birthday, the birthday cake and icing were black.

Bibliography

Amick, George. "Family May Be Nation's Finest." *Cincinnati Enquirer*, 1956.

Bakery. "Cincinnati Bakery Tour." "Schnecken take to the mail." February 1989.

Baking Buyer, the Bakers' Magazine. "Cake Town." November/December 2006.

Billman, Rebecca. "William Howard Thie, 73, operated Virginia Bakery." *Cincinnati Enquirer*, December 11, 1999.

Campbell, Polly. "Virginia Bakery's Schnecken Returns." *Cincinnati Enquirer*, October 31, 2006.

Chussler, George. "The 'Will Rogers' of Baking." ARBA *Fresh Baked*, November 1961.

Clopton, Willard. "No Retirement for Mrs. Thie." *Cincinnati Post and Times-Star*, 1960.

Driehaus, Bob. "Virginia Bakery to Close." *Cincinnati Post*, July 2000.

Eckberg, John. "The Daily Grind." *Cincinnati Enquirer*, November 20, 2005.

———. "Virginia Bakery Auctioned off Today." *Cincinnati Enquirer*, January 12, 2006.

Gerl, Ellen. "Ohio's Holiday Treats." *Ohio Magazine*, December/January 1999.

Gordon, Richard L. "Local Baker Heads Group of 5000 Bread Winners." *Cincinnati Post*, 1954.

Koewler, Mike. "Hear Ye, Hear Ye." *Valley Courier*, July 2009.

Laffoon, Polk IV. "Baker Thie's still in the thick of things." *Cincinnati Post*, April 20, 1977.

Lee, Edward, Denise Loeffler and Julie Rizer. "Nutrition Takes Center Stage at RBA/SBC Show." *Modern Baking*, June 1989.

Martin, Chuck. "Pastry Lovers Lose Old Friend." *Cincinnati Enquirer*, July 6, 2000.

———. "Sweet on Schnecken." *Cincinnati Enquirer*, September 12, 1999.

———. "Virginia Bakery Owners Switch to Wedding Cakes." *Cincinnati Enquirer*, October 15, 2000.

———. "Virginia Bakery Ready for Goodbye." *Cincinnati Enquirer*, July 16, 2000.

Modern Baking. "How Did Virginia Bakery Manage without Computers?" Leadership Award in Management, July 1995.

Paddleford, Clementine. "Grandma Thie's Coffee Cakes." *This Week*, September 1950.

Rieselman, Deborah. "Virginia Bakery Gets Fresh with Customers." *Clifton Living*, late 1980s.

Scott, Emily. "Baking the Bread of Life." *News Record*, June 1, 2000.

Stagaman, Mary. "Local Flavor." *Cincinnati Magazine*, June 2004.

———. "Snail Heaven." *Cincinnati Magazine*, October 1999.

St. Ursula Alumnae Spotlight. "Alum Makes Sweet Success after Family Bakery Closes." 2000.

Vitality News merchandising feature, a General Mills Publication. "Give the Customer What He Wants." 1960.

Index

A

about the recipes 92
almond roll-in 126
angel food cake 166
apple coffee cake 114

B

banana custard pie 175
brandy bumps 195
bran muffins 153
bread 198
  buttercrust 205
  cinnamon 206
  French 208
  general bread
     information 202
  hearth 208
  Vienna 208
  white 204
  whole wheat 206
bread ends 212
breakfast rolls 129
  butter Danish 136
  butterscotch gems 134
  cheese Danish 137
  cinnamon 132
  Danish pecan 133

Danish pecan crisps
    133
  double cinnamon 132
  filled Danish 136
  fruit Danish 137
  raisin 131
  sweet dough 131
brownies 151
brown-n-serve rolls 214
brown sugar 90
butter 90
butter bits 212
butter coffee cakes 111
buttercream filling 138
buttercream icing 143
buttercream pocket 124
buttercrust bread 205
butter Danish rolls 136
butter fans 214
butterscotch gems 134
butter wash 90

C

cakes 154
  angel food 166
  chocolate 163
  Dobash torte 164
  general cake
    information 161

  white 163
  yellow Windsor 162
cashew half moon
    cookies 192
cheesecake 149
cheese Danish rolls 137
cheese pocket 124
chess pie 172
chocolate cake 163
chocolate custard pie
    176
chocolate éclair 148
chocolate ganache 139
cinnamon bread 206
cinnamon crumbs 139
cinnamon rolls 132
cinnamon smear 140
cinnamon sugar 140
coconut custard pie 175
coffee cakes 106, 110
  apple 114
  butter 111
  cinnamon crumb 110
  grandma's bread 118
  Hungarian Bundt 116
  leaf loaf 117
  old-fashioned
    cinnamon 113
  plum 116

praline pecan 114
winky dink 113
cookies 183
  almond croissants 196
  brandy bumps 195
  cashew half moons
      192
  date nut kiss 196
  day and night 194
  French macaroons 193
  general cookie
      information 186
  Mexican wedding 190
  moon crescents 189
  nests 188
  shortbread 191
  shortbread sugar
      cutouts 191
  sugar 194
corn syrup 90
cream puffs 146
crullers 180
custard 147
custard pie filling 174
custard pies 174

D

Danish coffee cakes
  almond roll-in 126
  buttercream pocket
      124
  cheese pocket 124
  fruit pocket 123
  fruit roll-in 124
  plain tea ring 126
  royals 128
  seven sisters 122
Danish dough 119
Danish rolls
  butter 136
  butterscotch gems 134
  cheese 137
  filled 136
  fruit 137
  pecan 133

date nut kiss cookies 196
day and night cookies
      194
dinner rolls 210
  bread ends 212
  brown-n-serve 214
  butter bits 212
  butter fans 214
  hard rolls 216
  knots 215
  white roll dough 211
Dobash filling 165
Dobash torte 164
doneness 91
double cinnamon rolls
      132
doughnut glaze 140
doughnuts 177
  crullers 180
  Virginia reels 181
  yeast 179

E

éclairs 148
éclairs and cream puffs
      145
eggs 91
egg wash 91

F

filled Danish rolls 136
filled tea ring 127
fillings, frostings and
      other toppings
      138
  buttercream 138
  buttercream icing 143
  chess pie 172
  chocolate ganache 139
  cinnamon crumbs 139
  cinnamon smear 140
  cinnamon sugar 140
  custard pie 174
  Dobash 165

doughnut glaze 140
éclair and cream puff
      custard 147
  fruit filling 141
  fruit icing 141
  gem sugar 141
  glaze 142
  roll icing 142
  schnecken goo 142
  tea ring filling 143
  yellow crumbs 144
flour 91
French bread 208
French macaroon cookies
      193
front shop items 145
fruit Danish rolls 137
fruit filling 141
fruit-flavored icing 141
fruit roll-in 124

G

gem sugar 141
glaze 142
grandma's bread 118

H

hard rolls 216
hearth bread 208
Hungarian Bundt 116

K

knots 215

L

leaf loaf 117

M

Mexican wedding
      cookies 190
milk 92
moon crescent cookies
      189

N

nest cookies 188

O

old-fashioned
        cinnamon coffee
        cake 113

P

pan dressing 92
pan size 92
pastries
  bran muffins 153
  brownies 151
  cheesecake 149
  cream puffs 146
  éclair custard 147
  éclairs 148
pâte à choux 148
  Virginia reels 181
pecan crisps 133
pecan pie filling 173
pecan rolls 133
pies 167
  chess pie 172
  coconut custard 175
  custard 174
  dough 170
  pecan 173
  syrup 172
plain tea ring 126
plum coffee cake 116
praline pecan coffee cake
     114
proofing 92

R

raisin rolls 131
roll icing 142
royals: apple, blueberry
     and cherry 128

S

schnecken 95, 102
schnecken goo 142
seven sisters 122
shortbread dough 191
shortbread sugar cutouts
     191
sponge 204
sugar cookies 194
sweet dough breakfast
     rolls 131

T

tea ring filling 143
temperature 93

U

utensils 94

V

Vienna bread 208
Virginia reels 181

W

white bread 204
white bread sponge 204
white cake 163
white roll dough 211
whole wheat bread 206
winky dink coffee cake
     113

Y

yellow crumbs 144
yellow dough 109
yellow Windsor cake 162

About the Authors

Photo by Carly Thie.

Tom Thie was the last owner of Virginia Bakery, located in the historical Gaslight District of Clifton in Cincinnati, Ohio. He was raised in the suburb of White Oak but spent many of his early years in and around the bakery. After earning degrees from the Ohio State University and the prestigious Culinary Institute of America, where he graduated with honors, he went to work at several fine restaurants. He became a sous chef under Emeril Lagasse at Commander's Palace in New Orleans and opened the Phoenix restaurant in Cincinnati with Chef Paul Sturkey. He then took the helm at Virginia Bakery, which he ran for fifteen years. He now resides in White Oak with his daughter, Carly.

Cynthia Kuhn Beischel grew up in Clifton enjoying the Virginia Bakery products, which she actually took for granted. Only after the store closed and she was unable to match the delicious items she'd grown up with did she realize how really special their baked goods were. Her love of cookies and cakes, combined with her enjoyment of writing, made this project a perfect fit. Previously published work includes *Discover the Past*, a storybook about Cincinnati history that

Photo by Kristen Ungerecht.

encourages children and their families to enjoy learning about the past, and *From Eulogy to Joy*, a heartfelt anthology that explores the grieving process. Her educational background includes a bachelor of science in design at the University of Cincinnati and a master's degree in Montessori education from Xavier University. Cynthia resides with her two dogs in a quiet village north of Cincinnati, Ohio.